VAL U ABLE

VALUABLE

Linda S. Norwood

WESTBOW
PRESS
A DIVISION OF THOMAS NELSON

WestBow Press books may be ordered through booksellers or by contacting:
WestBow Press
A Division of Thomas Nelson
1663 Liberty Drive
Bloomington, IN 47403
www.westbowpress.com
1-(866) 928-1240

Because of the dynamic nature of the Internet, any web addresses or links contained in this book may have changed since publication and may no longer be valid. The views expressed in this work are solely those of the author and do not necessarily reflect the views of the publisher, and the publisher hereby disclaims any responsibility for them.

Any people depicted in stock imagery provided by Thinkstock are models, and such images are being used for illustrative purposes only. Certain stock imagery © Thinkstock.

Scripture quotations marked GW are from GOD'S WORD®, © 1995 God's Word to the Nations. Used by permission of Baker Publishing Group.

Scripture quotations marked (CEV) are from the Contemporary English Version Copyright © 1991,1992,1995 by American Bible Society, Used by Permission.

Scripture quotations marked GNB are from the Good News Translation in Today's English Version-Second Edition Copyright ©1992bby American Bible Society. Used by Permission.

Scripture quotations marked NASB are from the New American Standard Bible (NASB) Copyright ©1960, 1962, 1963, 1968, 1971, 1972, 1973, 1975, 1977, 1995 by The Lockman Foundation, La Habra, CA .All rights reserved. Used by Permission.

Scripture quotations marked ESV are from The Holy Bible, English Standard Version® (ESV®), copyright © 2001 by Crossway, a publishing ministry of Good News Publishers. Used by permission. All rights reserved.

Scripture quotations marked MSG are taken from The Message. Copyright © 1993, 1994, 1995, 1996, 2000, 2001, 2002. Used by permission of NavPress Publishing Group.

Scripture quotations marked AMP are taken from the Amplified® Bible, Copyright © 1954, 1958, 1962, 1964, 1965, 1987 by The Lockman Foundation Used by permission." (www.Lockman.org)

Scripture quotations marked KJV are from the King James Version of the Bible.

ISBN: 978-1-4497-5848-6 (sc)
ISBN: 978-1-4497-5847-9 (e)
Library of Congress Control Number: 2012912171

Printed in the United States of America
WestBow Press rev. date: 12/27/2012

To all who are experiencing hard places in life and feel inadequate. You need to know how precious you are and will always be in the sight and heart of God.

You are VALUABLE!

"There are many uncertainties in this life. God's love for you is not one of them."

CONTENTS

Part III Learn and Grow

PREFACE

Are you living a defeated life because of your own self-perception? Negative self-perception not only affects what you do, it also influences the way others see and treat you.

Self-esteem, or lack there of is at the core of what we do and why we do it. No matter your age, gender, social background, creed or nationality having a positive self-image is vital to move forward in life and to be able to set and achieve goals with success.

Healthy self-esteem is necessary for all human beings. Unfortunately, it is seen in a negative light when confused with arrogance or selfishness. In its proper context, self-esteem is not an "all about me" syndrome. It is about having a healthy love and appreciation for yourself as you learn to understand, embrace and enhance the qualities that make you uniquely who you are.

In April of 2010, a study on self-esteem reported results in the latest issue of the *Journal of Personality and Social Psychology*, published by the American Psychological Association. Amid the various findings, the study's lead author, Ulrich Orth, PhD states, "Self-esteem is related to better health, less criminal behavior, lower levels of depression and, overall, greater success in life."

However, recognizing your self-worth and appreciating who you are, can be a challenge with the bombardment of various media images society applauds as beautiful, which may look nothing like you.

Therefore, the premise of this book is that in God's eyes **you** and all of humanity are valuable because from His view you are a **V**ictorious **A**ccepted **L**oved **U**nderstood **A**ffirmed **B**lessed **L**iberated

Expression of His Grace. From this statement, we have the acronym **VALUABLE.**

VALUABLE is a three-part resource designed to assist with self-discovery, promote positive self-image and cultivate character. More importantly, **VALUABLE** will help develop your awareness of God's vast love for you through the study of His Word.

Part I, **Discovering Your Value**, examines Biblical truths to provide a sure foundation for healthy self-esteem.

The word of God is alive and active **(Heb 4:12 GW)**. It has the ability to effect positive change in the lives of all that will believe and include it in daily living. I believe that knowing and gaining insight into what God's Word says about you will have a significant impact on your life to cause transformation from the inside out, and teach you to value yourself as He does.

As we move forward together, you will see the words "self-image," "self-worth," and "self-esteem" used interchangeably.

ACKNOWLEDGEMENTS

To D. T. Mathis, who journeyed with me to read this manuscript, and provided her editorial expertise.

To W. Whittaker, M.D. who contributed her time and thoughts, as an experienced medical professional.

To my husband John who consistently exhibits patience and the practical wisdom of God that helps to keep me grounded.

To my gifted children, John Michael, Joshua and Nichel, who continually provide encouragement and support as the Lord enlarges my territory.

To my Mother Wilhelmenia Scott, who has always been a source of strength, love and encouragement while demonstrating what being a virtuous woman really means.

To the memory of my father, the late Rev. Dr. Otis Scott Sr. who left a legacy of faith, laughter, and the ability to see the glass half full.

To my sister Myrtle and brother Otis, who continue to love and encourage me in trusting in the sufficiency of God.

To Jackey, Cynthia, Tina, and Latoya my Heaven's Dew sisters, who labored with me in prayer for the completion of "VALUABLE".

Finally, to those whose names are not specifically mentioned here, who have encouraged me throughout the various seasons of my life and ministry.

You are VALUABLE!

VALUABLE

When I look in the mirror, what do I see?
Do I like who's looking back at me?

When I think of myself, what thoughts fill my mind?
Are they good, loving, patient and kind?

When I speak to myself, what words do I use?
Do they encourage, inspire or simply abuse?

Please listen my friend, listen today
His still small voice gently will say:

Valuable you are so precious to me
Valuable more than human eyes will ever see
You are so valuable worth more than silver or gold

Fearfully and wonderfully made
Yes, you are valuable.

PART I

Discovering Your Value

CHAPTER 1

Know Your Worth

When you hear the word "valuable," what images spring to your mind? Do you picture diamonds, gems and furs or a Mercedes-Benz? Perhaps you see an ample wardrobe of designer clothes and shoes or a wall lined with famous works of art.

Whatever you imagine probably does not include the face of your neighbor next door, the homeless person under the bridge or even your own face.

The word **valuable** has many definitions. As found in the Encarta Dictionary, they include: **1.**worth great deal of money **2.**having great importance or usefulness **3.**held dear, cherished or esteemed **4.**rare, highly prized because of being in short or limited supply.

Our society primarily attaches value to money. It is interesting to hear hosts on various entertainment programs discuss the "net worth" of famous people.

Curious about net worth, I gathered the following information from AARP on its website, www.aarp.org.
"Your net worth is the value of all of your assets, minus the total of all of your liabilities." Put another way, it is what you own minus what you owe.

In determining one's "net worth" owing more than you own is a negative net worth and owning more than you owe is a positive net worth.

The site listed things considered assets, such as: the current value of your home and other real estate; automobiles; household items; jewelry; retirement accounts; stocks; municipal bonds; mutual funds; savings bonds; cash value of life insurance; balances in checking and savings accounts; and cash.

As you can see, society calculates net worth by your material possessions. It is all about what you have and how much of it.

Frankly speaking, money is a necessity to live well in the earth. Earning an income is the reason people get up and head to their jobs. While there is nothing wrong with acquiring finances and owning possessions, they should not and indeed cannot determine a person's true value nor define who they are. Due to the transient nature of material things, it is always unwise to put trust in them because as it says in **Proverbs 23:5 GNB,** *Your money can be gone in a flash, as if it had grown wings and flown away like an eagle.*

(This is a truth particularly demonstrated in a difficult economy.)

There are longings of the heart and soul that acquiring things does not fulfill. Without balance in every area of life, just gaining the things our culture says we must have to make us happy can have the opposite effect.

Mark 8:36 from the Message translation is a very enlightening passage of scripture. It reads,

What good would it do to get everything you want and lose you, the real you?

The King James Version is probably more familiar.

For what shall it profit a man, if he shall gain the whole world, and lose his own soul?

In other words, what is the benefit of gathering all the wealth this world has to offer only to lose your sense of self, causing emotional instability and dysfunctional relationships? How much enjoyment does wealth really bring when your mind is in turmoil?

During days of economic upheaval, people face increasing stress, anxiety, and trauma, which often results in mental and emotional meltdowns. These issues, if left unresolved, can scar the soul where self-image is rooted.

Self-image is how you view yourself, including what you think or feel about yourself regularly. Understanding this provides deeper clarity on **Mark 8:36**. Material gain alone cannot replace peace, soundness of mind, dignity, or self-worth because self-worth and value do not come from a title, job, car, home, or what is in your bank account. Economic/social status in life makes you no more or less valuable in its true sense than another person. It is essential to be able to move into a place of knowing that as human beings we are all valuable.

> *Self-worth must be rooted in something beyond the measurement of the five physical senses.*

As we begin to walk with Godly self-confidence, our intrinsic value rises up and overflows to the outside, enabling us to become contributing members of excellence to our homes, churches, communities, and the world.

Think About It:

Society determines a person's worth by their material possession. However, self-worth must be rooted in something beyond the measurement of the five physical senses. It is essential to be able to move into a place of knowing that as human beings we are all valuable.

1. What currently determines your self-worth and value?

CHAPTER 2

The Power of Words

"Sticks and stones may break my bones but words will never hurt me". Most of us heard this old saying while growing up. In fact, we may have used it ourselves in retaliation to negative words said to or about us. Still, the truth of the matter is that words, whether positive or negative, do indeed affect us. Unfortunately, the negative ones tend to stick with us longer. It is amazing that if we receive five compliments and one criticism in a day, our tendency is to dwell on the one criticism.

Words, the main way in which people communicate, whether orally or written are powerful! They create images in the mind, evoke strong emotions, and attach memories to good and bad experiences, past and present.

Words guide the course of a person's life in a positive or negative direction. They can build up or tear down; hurt or bring healing; instill hope, faith or fear. **(James 3: 2, 5-6)**

Numerous scriptures paint a clear picture of the type of impact words carry. Here are a few examples to consider.

Job 4:3-4 (CEV)
Remember how your words have guided and encouraged many in need.

Psalms 52:2 GNB
You make plans to ruin others; your tongue is like a sharp razor. You are always inventing lies.

Psalms 64:3 (CEV)
Their words cut like swords, and their cruel remarks sting like sharp arrows.

Psalms 140:3 (CEV)
Their words bite deep like the poisonous fangs of a snake.

Proverbs 10:11a (CEV)
The words of good people are a source of life....

Proverbs 12:18 GNB
Thoughtless words can wound as deeply as any sword, but wisely spoken words can heal.

Proverbs 15:4 (CEV)
Kind words are good medicine, but deceitful words can really hurt.

Proverbs 18:21 (CEV)
Words can bring death or life! Talk too much, and you will eat everything you say.

As you can see, from the previous scriptures, the use of words is a serious matter. Depending on the words chosen, the results are wounds or healing; life or death; encouragement or discouragement.

None of us wants to be spoken to or about in a negative way. Yet if we are honest, we have said things that were hurtful or discouraging to or about someone else.
So when speaking, let us use wisdom being as concerned about what we say to others, as we are about what is said to us. Choose to allow your words to be a source of life.

Think About It

Words are the primary way people communicate and are powerful! They guide the course of a person's life in a positive or negative direction. Words can build up or tear down; hurt or bring healing; instill hope, faith or fear.

1. How are you using your words?

CHAPTER 3

Self-Talk=Self-Perception

As discussed in the previous chapter, words are powerful! Believing the things said to us early in life, as well as who said them, often affects the rest of our lives. Authority figures and others we admire, influence our self-esteem negatively or positively.

However, more important than the words and opinions of other people, are the self-talk words used that convey the thoughts and opinions you have of yourself which equate to your self-perception.

Read and think about these lines from the poem **Valuable**.

When I look in the mirror, what do I see?
Do I like whose looking back at me?

When I think of myself, what thoughts fill my mind?
Are they good, loving, patient and kind?

Do you frequently think negatively or positively about yourself? Take some "me" time and examine your thoughts.

Does a "grasshopper" mentality influence your thinking?

Numbers 3:33 Message

Why, we even saw the Nephilim giants... Alongside them we felt like grasshoppers.

Do not allow the "status", abilities or accomplishments of others make you feel inadequate.

When I speak to myself, what words do I use?
Do they encourage, inspire or simply abuse?

What are you speaking into your own life?
Remember the power of words. As it is important to speak positive words to others, it is also important to speak life and blessing over yourself.

Perhaps you are still lamenting over past mistakes living a life filled with regret. I can tell you first hand what a waste of time that is. Every person alive has missed the mark at some point (and some with alarming frequency).

Romans 3:23 (CEV)

(23) All of us have sinned and fallen short of God's glory.
You may have messed up big time, feeling guilty and ashamed for what you have done, or perhaps ashamed of something done to you. Whichever is the case, though not easy, it is essential to forgive.

Matthew 6:14 GNB

(14) "If you forgive others the wrongs they have done to you, your Father in heaven will also forgive you.
There is freedom for the one who forgives. When we forgive, we are open to receive the forgiveness we desperately need from the Lord.

1 John 1:9 GW

(9) God is faithful and reliable. If we confess our sins, he forgives them and cleanses us from everything we've done wrong.
Beating yourself up about the past is counterproductive, creating weight that keeps you from moving forward.

> *God does not hold our past against us.*
> *It is up to us to choose our future with Him.*

Philippians 3:13-14 KJV
(13) ... but this one thing I do, forgetting those things which are behind, and reaching forth unto those things which are before,
(14) I press toward the mark for the prize of the high calling of God in Christ Jesus.
God created you with destiny in mind. Seek Him and go for it! Learn from mistakes while leaving the past right where it belongs: in the past.
Through Christ Jesus, we have as many fresh starts as we need! Forgiving ourselves as well as others, imparts the freedom needed to move forward.

Think About It

Self-talk words convey the thoughts and opinions you have of yourself which equate to your self-perception.
Beating yourself up about the past is counterproductive. Learn from your mistakes, be quick to forgive yourself and others then move forward.

1. Are you able to forgive yourself and others for past mistakes?

CHAPTER 4

Secure Your Identity

There is more to one's identity than a name given at birth. A person's name/identity involves their character and reputation, as well as affects their mobility in society. Consequently, identity is quite important.

In our society, identity theft is a crime. As defined on the Federal Trade Commission's (FTC) website, federaltradecommission.com, identity theft involves the use of a person's name, social security number, or credit card without their permission to commit fraud and other criminal acts. The FTC estimates that as many as nine million Americans have their identities stolen each year. It is highly probable that you and I or someone we know may have experienced some form of identity theft. Usually, the way we find out is through the review of our credit card statement or credit report.

Identity theft is serious because, whether a victim is able to have the problem resolved quickly with minimal expense, or spends a lot of time and money trying to repair their credit, the damage done to their "good" name may be more difficult to repair. Consequently, a person may discover that attempts to further their education, buy a home, car or other major purchase, even future employment becomes problematic.

As identity theft is a serious problem in our natural lives, so too is the threat we face spiritually.

Our enemy Satan tries to bring doubt, desperation and despair into our lives with thoughts of worthlessness and failure.

He uses confusion about who we are and our purpose in life to derail the good plans God has for us (**Jeremiah 29:11**). It is during those times of identity crises if not mindful, a person may engage in self-destructive behavior. Trying quick fixes of sex, alcohol, marijuana, cocaine and other drugs, illegal or prescribed, will not fill the emptiness or provide lasting satisfaction and confidence.

Self-worth is defined as confidence in personal value and worth as an individual to also encompass beliefs, emotions and behavior.
Words and behavior are connected to the attitudes and thoughts deeply rooted in the beliefs and values of the heart. What you believe; how you think and feel about yourself is a determining factor in the degree of your success in life, because actions follow thoughts.

What you do routinely is a strong indicator of your self-esteem.

Stop and think for a moment.
Are you abusing your body in some way with the use of drugs, alcohol, or even food as self-medication in an attempt to mask feelings of inadequacy? Has verbal, emotional, or even physical abuse from others been a way of life for you because it is what you believe you deserve?
Well, nothing could be farther from the truth. Other people's opinions, attitudes and actions do not define who you are nor do they determine your worth. Likewise, do not allow your own faulty thinking or previous negative experiences cause you to devalue yourself and keep you from reaching your full potential. Realize that you are VALUABLE!

Genesis, the first book of the Old Testament, is the book of beginnings. The first chapter establishes the creation and identity of human beings as well as God's plan for humanity. Take time to read these two verses for yourself.

Genesis 1:26–27 GW

26) Then God said, "Let us make humans in our image, in our likeness. Let them rule the fish in the sea, the birds in the sky, the domestic animals all over the earth, and all the animals that crawl on the earth."
27) So God created humans in his image. In the image of God he created them. He created them male and female.

God established from the beginning that all human beings were valuable when He created the first man and woman in His own image. Therefore, awareness (knowledge) of being a special creation made in the image and likeness of your Heavenly Father is important to safeguard against a negative self-image and secure your identity.

Think About It

What you believe; how you think and feel about yourself is a determining factor in the degree of your success in life, because actions follow thoughts. Do not allow your own faulty thinking or previous negative experiences cause you to devalue yourself and keep you from reaching your full potential.

1. Do you feel that your identity is secure?

CHAPTER 5

Fearfully and Wonderfully Made

When God created the first man and woman, a different process took place because He intended for us to stand out from the rest of His creation.

In **Genesis 1:26a GW,** as with other creations, He spoke *Then God said, "Let us make humans in our image, in our likeness...* but also physically involved Himself in the creation of man. **Genesis 2:7a MSG** *GOD formed Man out of dirt from the ground...* The creation of woman was intimate and unique. **Genesis 2:21-22 GNB**

Then the LORD God made the man fall into a deep sleep, and while he was sleeping, He took out one of the man's ribs and closed up the flesh.

He formed a woman out of the rib and brought her to him.

At that moment, God established a pattern that demonstrated His desire to be personally involved in the lives of people for all time!

The particular care God used when He created man and woman was an unparalleled feat!

The Psalmist David had this revelation,

Psalms 139:14 ESV *I praise you, for I am fearfully and wonderfully made. Wonderful are your works; my soul knows it very well.*

God carefully constructed and formed man's physical body with His own hands, and then blew His very own God breath or Spirit into that form. He created us to be like Him on the inside.

Just as God is triune existing as Father, Son and Holy Spirit, He created humans spirit, soul and body.
(I Thessalonians 5:23.)

With the **body,** we make contact with and interact in the world using the five physical senses of taste, touch, vision, smell, and hearing. It is what we need to operate effectively in the earth. It will die, and over time return to dust.

Take a moment and reflect on how intricate and complex the human body is with its systems such as the circulatory, respiratory, immune, musculoskeletal and digestive, to name a few. It is amazing that these systems, with our various internal organs, function without us thinking about them. The way our bodies function is truly miraculous!

The **soul,** while sometimes interchanged with the spirit, is distinct. It is where the activities of the _mind or intellect_ ability to think and reason; the _will_ exercising choice and making decisions; and _emotions_ what and how we feel, take place. The soul being immortal will be active throughout eternity.

It is through our **spirit,** that we are able to connect with God. It is very real but is invisible, intangible and immortal. The Hebrew word for spirit is _ruach,_ often translated as breath. Without the spirit, the physical body is dead. Read this passage from **Genesis 2:7 GNB.**

(7) Then the LORD God took some soil from the ground and formed a man out of it; he breathed life-giving breath into his nostrils and the man began to live.

The body of man was completely formed but not alive until God breathed into it.

When God's breath flowed into man, he became alive and aware, spirit, soul and body with the ability to think reason and speak.

This creative process by God, along with the vast ability He placed in human beings, is what set us apart from all other creation. We are distinguished and valuable because we are God's creation!

Think About It

God created humans in His image and likeness.

The particular care God used when He created man and woman was an unparalleled feat!

Just as God is triune existing as Father, Son and Holy Spirit, He created humans spirit, soul and body setting us apart from the rest of His creation.

1. What does being fearfully and wonderfully made mean to you?

CHAPTER 6

What Makes Us Tick?

The nature of human beings has been an interesting study for centuries. As a former educator, I learned about different theories of various psychologists regarding human development. Psychology involves the scientific study of the human mind endeavoring to understand and explain thought, emotion and behavior. In other words, it attempts to figure out what "makes us tick."

I conducted research on the website www.psychology.about.com to include information on "Hierarchy of Needs", a theory introduced by psychologist, Abraham Maslow. His humanistic approach to psychology focused on individual potential and stressed the importance of growth and self-actualization. This approach credits the individual more for being in control of and determining their state of mental health.

Maslow's theory consists of five levels of human needs from one being the lowest, to five as the highest. In his model, usually represented as a pyramid, physical needs serve as the base with the other category of needs building upon the satisfaction of prior needs.

Take a moment to examine his list.

---

1. **Physical needs** = the basic things necessary to sustain life. Examples include air, food, water and sleep
2. **Security needs** = the things that help people feel secure. Examples include shelter, employment, and a safe environment
3. **Social needs** = relationships, love, affection, sense of belonging
4. **Esteem needs** = self-esteem, personal worth, social recognition and accomplishment
5. **Self-Actualizing needs** = being self-aware, concerned with personal growth and fulfilling own potential, less worried about the opinion of others

---

I believe God allowed Maslow and other psychologists to gain some insight into aspects of human development and behavior.
Whether or not you agree with Maslow's psychological approach, it is evident that from birth to death, all people have needs that change based on where they are in life.

A sense of feeling appreciated and valued is something all people want to experience and need. Unfortunately, the methods used, depending on what they are to meet this need, can cause more damage than the need going un-met by others. Even so, as air, food, and water are necessary to sustain the physical body, self-esteem is necessary to one's mental well-being; but where does it come from? How do we attain and hang on to our self-esteem? To some, the answer is **total reliance** on human willpower, natural ability, and external accomplishments.

Navigating through life, we encounter situations too big to handle on our own that truthfully, God never intended for us to. I have come to realize that, **despite great human potential, exceptional ability**

and determination, we definitely need God's help to actually reach our full potential.

Everything that makes us healthy functioning humans, including our potential, desires etc., God our Creator placed in us to become our best selves. I am so glad He knows and understands exactly what we need.

Not only does God know exactly what we need; in His sovereignty, He has also given us a place of authority none other of His creation holds. Down deep inside of people is a desire to be in charge.

A Place of Authority

When you watch little children play on the playground, several want to be the "boss." We see it in both males and females. What is the reason for this tendency? Yes, this drive is stronger and more apparent in certain personality types than in others, but it is there nonetheless.

Why is it there? We find the answer in **Genesis 1:26-28 GW.**

(26) Then God said, "Let us make humans in our image, in our likeness. Let them rule the fish in the sea, the birds in the sky, the domestic animals all over the earth, and all the animals that crawl on the earth."

(27) So God created humans in his image. In the image of God he created them. He created them male and female.

(28) God blessed them and said, "Be fertile, increase in number, fill the earth, and be its master. Rule the fish in the sea, the birds in the sky, and all the animals that crawl on the earth."

The previous passages are rich with enlightening truth.

God created humans then spoke blessing and dominion into the very fabric of their being. The man and woman were to be partners in ruling over His creation, but remain under God's ultimate authority.

The following Psalm extols the greatness of God while verses 4-6 provide confirmation as to the place of authority God purposed us to occupy.

Psalms 8:1-9 GNB

1. O LORD, our Lord, your greatness is seen in all the world! Your praise reaches up to the heavens;

2. it is sung by children and babies. You are safe and secure from all your enemies; you stop anyone who opposes you.

3. When I look at the sky, which you have made, at the moon and the stars, which you set in their places---

4. what are human beings, that you think of them; mere mortals, that you care for them?

*5. **Yet you made them inferior only to yourself; you crowned them with glory and honor.***

*6. **You appointed them rulers over everything you made; you placed them over all creation:***

7. sheep and cattle, and the wild animals too;

8. the birds and the fish and the creatures in the seas.

9. O LORD, our Lord, your greatness is seen in all the world!

According to what we have seen in scripture, God's plan from the beginning was for humans to subdue and oversee the earth. He gave them dominion over all animals, birds and fish. However, that dominion was never to be over other people nor was man's oversight of the earth to be in isolation from God.

He desires fellowship with us because of all the marvelous creations made, He delights in us the most!

We are much more than priceless works of art.

Art collectors pay huge sums of money to purchase what they consider valuable pieces of art. Typically, the artwork beautifully displayed, remains enjoyed from afar. The perception is that handling something precious causes its value to diminish.

For example, the value of the most expensive of luxury cars depreciates when driven off the lot, much to the dismay of the car owner.

While some objects lose their value, it is not the case with people, because God created us. He created us to interact with Him and with one another. *The more interaction we have with God, allowing Him complete access to our lives, the more valuable we become. Our value increases in ways that enables us to have a positive influence in the lives of others.*

Think About It

All people have needs that change based on where they are in life. Appreciation and value contributes to healthy self-esteem and is something we all want to experience and need.

God our Creator placed everything on the inside of us that makes us healthy functioning humans. He also spoke blessing and dominion into the very fabric of our being at creation because He originally planned for us to rule over the earth, but remain under His ultimate authority.

Giving God complete access to our lives causes our value to increase.

1. What are you trying to manage or accomplish in your own strength?

CHAPTER 7

The Choice

Perhaps some may wonder if God created, blessed and gave humans authority to rule, then why we are such a mess.

When what God created to be good becomes perverted or twisted, the results are a horrible mess.

Remember in an earlier chapter we talked about God creating humanity with the ability to choose. There are always consequences when we exert our will to make choices. Our actions will be foolish or wise depending on whose voice we choose to follow.

Let me tell you a little story.

There once was an extremely wealthy and powerful man named Mr. Gee who owned a tremendous amount of property. Though this man possessed great wealth and power, he also possessed a very generous loving heart.

One day after reviewing all of his assets, he decided that sharing what he had would increase his satisfaction/happiness. He thought about all of the real estate he owned, chose the best acres on which to build an estate then drew up architectural plans for the landscape including buildings he wanted on the property.

Upon completion, he looked at everything with a satisfied eye. An assortment of stately trees lined the perimeter of the well-manicured estate. Within lay an exquisite botanical garden of rare beautiful plant life.

Surrounding the garden were two ponds: one filled with a variety of tropical fish to enjoy, the other containing fish to catch and eat if desired. A magnificent fountain in the center of the garden flowed with sparkling water that danced as the sunlight hit it. Yes, indeed, all of it was something glorious to behold!

The mansion built contained every convenience imaginable. It was energy efficient, replete with state of the art technology. All it lacked was an occupant.

After reviewing the results from different background checks, Mr. Gee chose a married couple, Alex and Emma Peoples, from his list. Given the size of the estate, Mr. Gee believed the two of them would oversee the management aspects better than one.

Each had the qualities he desired and capacity to run the estate effectively. However, there were important ground rules of the estate to establish with them as to what he expected; things he desired to impart to them as well as share with them.

He planned to take his time familiarizing them with their new environment and communicate his thoughts for upcoming businesses to incorporate as part of the estate.

Mr. Gee made evening visits and shared his heart with them giving them full authority to make decisions concerning the estate in his stead. They had full charge of everything except one small area Mr. Gee reserved for himself. Therefore, Alex and Emma had a directive to leave that area alone warning of dire consequences if they did not.

Despite the warning, they disobeyed Mr. Gee due to a negative influence. A disgruntled former employee of Mr. Gee named Sam, decided to visit the estate upon learning of Mr. Gee's improvements. Emma, after talking with Sam, decided that spot would be perfect for a little herb garden she wanted to plant. As he pointed out, the land looked extremely rich and fertile with a nice little stream flowing nearby. She actually had not paid much attention to it before talking to Sam, but had to agree it **looked** enticing. Alex, while not completely sold on the idea, chose to go along with Emma not risking the possibility sleepless nights on their couch. With that, they began to work on the garden. As Alex and Emma dug their shovels into the rich soil, they began to feel very uneasy.

Unknown to Alex or Emma, Sam took every opportunity he could to undermine Mr. Gee. He coveted the estate and felt he should be the one running it. Truth is, years back, Mr. Gee placed Sam in charge of a major project and he did a great job at first. However, after a while Sam made the mistake of allowing the accolades go to his the head. He grew dissatisfied with position he had, beginning to think that he knew more, and could run the company better than Mr. Gee himself.

He and the others that supported him received an immediate and irrevocable demotion. He became an underling, performing menial tasks that were blows to his inordinate pride. Sam decided that if he could not be in charge of the estate, he would cause trouble for anyone who was. Not overtly though, but cunningly and these folks were ripe for the picking. Actually, he had been a little surprised Alex had not shut him down when he suggested Emma pay more attention to that precious little strip of property "the boss" told them to leave alone.

When Mr. Gee came for his visit that evening, he could tell immediately that something was wrong. His heart sank and tears filled his eyes when he thought about what had to happen.

If you were Mr. Gee, what would you do?

Think About It

God created humans with the ability to think, reason, and make choices. Positive or negative consequences are the result of the choices we make. Choosing to disobey God always causes problems.

1. Have your recent choices been wise or foolish?

CHAPTER 8

God's View of You

I hope you found the scenario from the previous chapter enjoyable and thought provoking. However, a real situation took place found in **Genesis 2:3- 3:24** that caused the problems we have today. As you read this account for yourselves, you will discover that the man and woman's disobedience stripped them of dignity, confidence, authority and fellowship with God.

The scope of their actions caused a major rift (referred to as the fall of man) between all subsequent humanity and their Creator.

Yet, God's view of humanity did not change. The man and woman were still very important to Him and He already had a plan for their welfare and all of humanity in place. Remember in **Psalm 8:5** God crowned them with glory. The glory of God was their covering therefore; it is why they were naked and initially unashamed. **(Genesis 2:25)**

In the beginning, the couple looked forward to the presence of God but after sin, the glory of God departed leaving them exposed. As a result, fear entered in making them self-conscious trying to hide from God as well as each other. They had indeed fallen short of God's glory!

Therefore, restoration could and would take place only one way.

John 3:16-17 GNB

(16) For God loved the world so much that he gave his only Son, so that everyone who believes in him may not die but have eternal life.
(17) For God did not send his Son into the world to be its judge, but to be its savior.

Romans 3:23-25 (CEV)

(23) All of us have sinned and fallen short of God's glory.
(24) But God treats us much better than we deserve, and because of Christ Jesus, he freely accepts us and sets us free from our sins.
(25) God sent Christ to be our sacrifice. Christ offered his life's blood, so that by faith in him we could come to God. And God did this to show that in the past he was right to be patient and forgive sinners. This also shows that God is right when he <u>accepts</u> people who have faith in Jesus.

Because of the sin of Adam (man), **all** of humanity received a death sentence; **but because of Jesus**, the price was paid and hope restored for all people.
Even with the fall of humanity, God's love remained full and strong!

Romans 5:17-19 GNB.

(17) It is true that through the sin of one man death began to rule because of that one man. But how much greater is the result of what was done by the one man, Jesus Christ! All who receive God's abundant grace and are freely put right with him will rule in life through Christ.
(18) So then, as the one sin condemned all people, in the same way the one righteous act sets all people free and gives them life.
(19) And just as all people were made sinners as the result of the disobedience of one man, in the same way they will all be put right with God as the result of the obedience of the one man.

It is truly wonderful that God made a way to redeem and restore us through His Son Jesus!
Jesus is the reason God views each of us as a:
Victorious, **A**ccepted, **L**oved, **U**nderstood, **A**ffirmed, **B**lessed, **L**iberated, **E**xpression of His grace

We are all **VALUABLE** to Him!

> ## Titus 2:11 GNB *For God has revealed his grace for the salvation of all people.*

God desires a real love relationship with all people. It is not about rules and regulations. It is absolutely about the RELATIONSHIP afforded to us by **His grace**.

***John 1:17* GNB** *God gave the Law through Moses, but grace and truth came through Jesus Christ.*

Romans 3:24 GNB *But by the free gift of God's grace all are put right with him through Christ Jesus, who sets them free.*

Through our relationship with Him, we have a lasting confidence and true sense of worth.

If you have not yet given your life to Jesus accepting Him as your personal Savior and Lord, you are extremely important and loved by God as confirmed in **Romans 5:8 GNB.**

(8) But God has shown us how much he loves us---it was while we were still sinners that Christ died for us!

Jesus paid the price for all, but salvation is not automatic; nor is it passed on from our parents or others. Each person must choose to accept it.

Salvation defined*: is the state of being saved; protected from harm, risk, loss, destruction etc.*

From a Theological Perspective, *it is deliverance from the power and penalty of sin; redemption.*

As discussed in Chapter 4, we are spirit; have a soul and live in a body. Our spirit and soul will live on throughout eternity. The question is where. Scripture tells us that we will be with God happy forever or apart from Him in torment. (**Matthew 25:46**)

Salvation in spiritual terms, mean we will spend eternity with the Lord. That is great news, but again it is up to each person to accept God's provision.

These definitions of the word *accept* get right to the point.

<u>*Accept*</u>
1. To take something offered, e.g. a gift or payment
John 3:16-17 GNB
(16) For God loved the world so much that he gave his only Son

2. Say yes to an invitation or offer
Romans 5:17
.....All who receive God's abundant grace and are freely put right with him will rule in life through Christ.

3. To acknowledge a fact or truth and come to terms with it
Romans 3:23-25 (CEV)
(23) All of us have sinned and fallen short of God's glory.

You can think of salvation this way. When a postal worker comes to your door with a special delivery with your name on it, you have to accept the package if you want it. The postal worker will then require your signature to verify your acceptance.

Where salvation is concerned, this is the way to receive your package:

Romans 10:9N-11 GNB
(9) If you confess that Jesus is Lord and believe that God raised him from death, you will be saved.
(10) For it is by our faith that we are put right with God; it is by our confession that we are saved.
(11) The scripture says, "Whoever believes in him will not be disappointed."

You were **so valuable** that God gave His very best when He gave Jesus to be the Redeemer. God does not require you to get everything right before coming to Him. Just receive the priceless gift of salvation offered through Jesus today. He is waiting on you with open arms.

Think About It

God desires a real love relationship with all people that is not according to rules, regulations and their behavior but is absolutely by His grace. God does not require you to get everything right before coming to Him. He has extended the gift of salvation to all willing to receive it through His Son Jesus.

1. Do you need to accept your package of salvation and embrace your value?

If the answer is yes, please pray this:
Jesus, I want the fullness of salvation. I turn from my sins and ask you to live in me today. I surrender my will to yours and make you my Lord. Thank You for giving me a brand new life of value filled with purpose! Amen

Never forget you are **VALUABLE**!

Notes

Notes

PART II

Insight and Reflections

God views you as a:

Victorious, **A**ccepted, **L**oved, **U**nderstood, **A**ffirmed, **B**lessed, **L**iberated, **E**xpression of His grace

INTRODUCTION

God's view of humanity, particularly all who believe in His son, Jesus the Christ, is through His finished work on the cross.
Jesus' sacrificial death paid the price for the sins of the entire world.

Part II, **Insight and Reflections** provides corresponding scriptures to accompany the definition of each word in the acronym. The scriptures reveal God's heart of love toward His people.

You will have room to jot down your impressions and thoughts as you go through each word of the acronym, VALUABLE.

From God's view you are:

VICTORIOUS

Succeeding in
Overcoming a
Difficult situation
Or an obstacle

1 Corinthians 15:57-58 GNB
57. But thanks be to God who gives us the victory through our Lord Jesus Christ!
58. So then, my dear friends, stand firm and steady. Keep busy always in your work for the Lord, since you know that nothing you do in the Lord's service is ever useless.

Romans 8:37 CEV In everything we have won more than a victory because of Christ who loves us.

Valuable Insight

Stay encouraged in spite of your feelings, situations, or circumstances. Jesus has assured victory to all who believe and trust in Him. Walk in it today!

~Reflect on living victoriously in Christ ~

_____

_____

_____

_____

_____

_____

_____

_____

From God's view you are:

```
┌─────────────────────────────────────────┐
│              ACCEPTED                     │
│           Be welcomed as                  │
│         A member of a group;              │
│        Have a sense of belonging          │
└─────────────────────────────────────────┘
```

Romans 4:24 (CEV) They were written for us, since we will also be accepted because of our faith in God, who raised our Lord Jesus to life.

Romans 5:17 (CEV) Death ruled like a king because Adam had sinned. But that cannot compare with what Jesus Christ has done. God has been so kind to us, and he has accepted us because of Jesus. And so we will live and rule like kings.

Valuable Insight

Every human born in this world desires a sense of belonging. This desire can lead to unwise decisions and associations. Know that God, Creator of the universe, calls you His very own.

~Reflect on being accepted by God~

_____

_____

_____

_____

_____

_____

_____

_____

_____

_____

From God's view you are:

LOVED
Shown kindness, tender affection
And compassion

Ephesians 2:4 GW But God is rich in mercy because of his great love for us.

(Romans 8:38-39 CEV) I am sure that nothing can separate us from God's love--not life or death, not angels or spirits, not the present or the future, and not powers above or powers below. Nothing in all creation can separate us from God's love for us in Christ Jesus our Lord!

Valuable Insight

God is love. His love toward us is unconditional and everlasting. Nothing we do will ever cause Him to stop loving us.

~Reflect on God's unconditional love for you ~

_____

_____

_____

_____

_____

_____

_____

_____

_____

_____

From God's view you are:

> # UNDERSTOOD
>
> *Known; One's character*
> *Recognized especially in a*
> *Sympathetic, tolerant,*
> *Or empathetic way*

Psalms 103:14 MSG He knows us inside and out, keeps in mind that we're made of mud.

Hebrews 4:15 GW We have a chief priest who is able to sympathize with our weaknesses. He was tempted in every way that we are, but he didn't sin.

Valuable Insight

As we experience trouble in life, it is easy to think that no one knows how we feel or understands what we are going through. While others may or may not be able to relate to our issues, it is reassuring to know that Jesus totally understands everything about us including our feelings.

~Reflect on knowing that when no one
else understands you, God does~

_____

_____

_____

_____

_____

_____

_____

_____

_____

From God's view you are:

AFFIRMED

*To declare support
For somebody or something;
Acknowledgement*

Isaiah 41:10 GW Don't be afraid, because I am with you. Don't be intimidated; I am your God. I will strengthen you. I will help you. I will support you with my victorious right hand.

Isaiah 46:4 GW Even when you're old, I'll take care of you. Even when your hair turns gray, I'll support you. I made you and will continue to care for you. I'll support you and save you.

Valuable Insight

Receiving affirmation from someone greatly regarded, contributes much to a person's self-esteem. Although support from people is reassuring, much more sustaining is the affirmation God provides to all who put their trust in Him.

~Reflect on knowing you are affirmed by God~

_____

_____

_____

_____

_____

_____

_____

_____

_____

From God's view you are:

> # BLESSED
> *Happy; prosperous in worldly affairs;*
> *Enjoying spiritual happiness*
> *and the favor of God*

Genesis 5:1b-2 GW ...When God created humans, he made them in the likeness of God. **2.** He created them male and female. He blessed them and called them humans when he created them.

Ephesians 1:3 GW Praise the God and Father of our Lord Jesus Christ! Through Christ, God has blessed us with every spiritual blessing that heaven has to offer.

Valuable Insight

God's kind intent has always been to bless His people. When sin occurred in the garden and judgment pronounced upon the man and woman, God already had a plan to restore humanity. Jesus bore the curse at Calvary providing the avenue for us to enjoy the blessing of God as intended. (Gal 3:13-14)

~Reflect on God's intent for you to prosper~

_____

_____

_____

_____

_____

_____

_____

_____

From God's view you are:

LIBERATED

Released or rescued from being physically bound,
Or from being confined, enslaved, captured,
Or imprisoned

Galatians 5:1 GW Christ has freed us so that we may enjoy the benefits of freedom. Therefore, be firm in this freedom, and don't become slaves again.

Romans 8:2 ESV For the law of the Spirit of life has set you free in Christ Jesus from the law of sin and death.

Valuable Insight'

Liberty is a wonderful thing that many people take for granted. However, liberty has always come with a price. Jesus' shed blood paid the price to rescue all held captive to sin spiritually, emotionally and physically. Receive your freedom today!

~Reflect on living free from the bondage of sin~

_____
_____
_____
_____
_____
_____
_____
_____
_____

From God's view, you are an:

EXPRESSION OF HIS GRACE

*An illustration or representation of
grace: favor; good will; kindness;
mercy; pardon;*

Romans 5:17 GNB It is true that through the sin of one man death began to rule because of that one man. But how much greater is the result of what was done by the one man, Jesus Christ! All who receive God's abundant grace and are freely put right with him will rule in life through Christ.

Ephesians 1:6–7a GNB Let us praise God for his glorious grace, for the free gift he gave us in his dear Son! **7.** For by the blood of Christ we are set free, that is, our sins are forgiven.

Valuable Insight

Grace is more than words said before a meal. Grace is a tremendous gift from God that encompasses His favor and loving kindness. By God's grace we are forgiven when we fall short. Because Jesus established peace between God and humanity, we truly illustrate God's good will in the earth.

~Reflect on the privilege of being an
expression of God's grace~

_____

_____

_____

_____

_____

_____

PART III

Learn and Grow

INTRODUCTION

In Part I &II of "**VALUABLE**," the acronym expressed God's heart toward you. I pray that as you reflected on each word and meaning in the acronym, you were able to recognize your importance to Him and now have a more favorable view of yourself and others.

The quote, "God loves us just the way we are, but too much to leave us that way" speaks volumes. Granting that it is important not to beat ourselves up regarding where we fall short, it also important, not to settle with where we are. All of us are works in progress, with areas that need improvement. I hope we are willing to do what we can, to grow as individuals. Continuing on our journey, we will discuss **VALUABLE** in a different way trusting God's Holy Spirit to help us become greater assets to the Kingdom of God thereby, exerting godly influence in the earth.

Part III, **Learn and Grow** will look at being **VALUABLE** through the lens of the words **V**irtue, **A**uthentic, **L**ove, **U**nique, **A**bide, **B**alance, **L**egacy and **E**ndurance.

The purpose of each lesson utilizing these words is to:
- **Expand your thinking**
- **Help you cultivate positive traits**
- **Impart biblical principles relevant for daily living.**

Moving forward, I pray that as you learn and grow personally, you are encouraged as well as equipped to enrich the lives of others.

LESSON 1

VIRTUE

Moral excellence; a particular beneficial quality: advantage; Effective power

Virtue is a word infrequently used, but greatly needed in our society. It incorporates strength; excellence in behavior- doing what is right because it is the right thing to do; effectiveness- the ability to produce a desired outcome or result.

Virtue is a quality that has a positive effect on others.

Proverbs 31 presents an example of a woman whose life displays virtue in action. In other Bible translations, renderings of the word virtue include good, capable, strong character, and worth. Each word fits the previous definition. The following verses reveal why she is a valuable woman. Whether real or symbolic, her character and behavior shine like a beacon providing rich lessons we can learn. Read the passage below.

Proverbs 31:10-31 GNB
(10) How hard it is to find a capable wife! She is worth far more than jewels!
(11) Her husband puts his confidence in her, and he will never be poor.
(12) As long as she lives, she does him good and never harm.
(13) She keeps herself busy making wool and linen cloth.
(14) She brings home food from out-of-the-way places, as merchant ships do.
(15) She gets up before daylight to prepare food for her family and to tell her servant women what to do.
(16) She looks at land and buys it, and with money she has earned she plants a vineyard.
(17) She is a hard worker, strong and industrious.

(18) She knows the value of everything she makes, and works late into the night.

(19) She spins her own thread and weaves her own cloth.

(20) She is generous to the poor and needy.

(21) She doesn't worry when it snows, because her family has warm clothing.

(22) She makes bedspreads and wears clothes of fine purple linen.

(23) Her husband is well known, one of the leading citizens.

(24) She makes clothes and belts, and sells them to merchants.

(25) She is strong and respected and not afraid of the future.

(26) She speaks with a gentle wisdom.

(27) She is always busy and looks after her family's needs.

(28) Her children show their appreciation, and her husband praises her.

(29) He says, "Many women are good wives, but you are the best of them all."

(30) Charm is deceptive and beauty disappears, but a woman who honors the LORD should be praised.

(31) Give her credit for all she does. She deserves the respect of everyone.

Observations

As I studied this woman, I discovered the following things about her.

Verse 10- Rare
- precious, uncommon

Verse 11&12- Trustworthy
- a trustworthy asset to her husband
- actions don't drain household resources rather builds them up
- she is good to her husband treating him with respect
- her husband has complete confidence in her

Verse 13-15- Industrious
- keeps busy; engages in positive and productive activities that help to provide for the family

- is an early riser to prepare for the day; sees to needs of her family
- demonstrates ability to lead by giving instructions to the people that work for her; keeps household in order

Verse 16-19- Resourceful
- has an eye for quality products and makes wise investments
- owns profitable business and real estate; works hard knows and appreciates what she has, recognizes and values her own worth and creativity

Verse 20-21- Benevolent
- is compassionate and generous, helps those less fortunate
- does not worry
- is prepared for adverse conditions

Verse 22-24- Accomplished
- good at what she does, has poise, dignity and style
- her positive actions/lifestyle instrumental to the success of husband
- has good reputation in community, strong and influential, she and husband well respected

Verse 25- Confident/Resilient
- strong
- unafraid, takes each day as it comes

Verse 26- Wise
- knows when to speak, what to say, and how to say it.

Verse 28-29- Valued
- appreciated and admired by her children
- praised and cherished by husband

Verse 30- Reverent
- honors God

Verse 31- Commended
- deserves acclaim and respect for all she does

Let's Chat

WOW! What an amazing woman! Having the ability to do all those things not only seems intimidating, but exhausting also.

Do not get discouraged if you have not arrived at that place yet. Neither have I. All of us are works in progress. Whether or not this woman was real or an ideal, the scripture contains gems that if properly developed, will enrich every area of our lives.
However, let me emphasize that living a virtuous life is **not** developing a SUPERWOMAN or MAN (men should display virtue as well) syndrome, rather, it is about walking in **your** full potential. Because this woman used her gifts, talents and abilities, she, her family and household were able to profit. Additionally, she was in position to help others in need.
Her lifestyle earned admiration, praise, and respect from her family and the community. Her self-esteem was high because she did her best with a clear understanding of her who she was.

This woman of virtue probably did not get there overnight. As we take one-step at a time, day by day, we too, will be the people of virtue God intends for us to be.
While we should not become lazy, a flurry of activity is not the goal. Try to look beyond all the activities and into her heart.

This woman's heart motive was to ensure the wellbeing of her family, household and to honor God.
In my opinion, verse 30 is the secret to her success.
Because of her heart for God (desiring to honor Him), she had His power working in her life, bringing her honor and respect in return.
This is a biblical principle found in **1 Samuel 2:30 ESV**
30 **Therefore the LORD the God of Israel declares: …. those who honor me I will honor, and those who despise me shall be lightly esteemed.**
I am continually amazed and encouraged by God's Word. God gives honor to those who honor Him. Individuals that do not respect God

Linda S. Norwood

do not enjoy the same degree of regard, but have value because of His tremendous love.

Work It Out

~Review Proverbs 31:10-31 from the lesson.

Match the verse that best demonstrates the qualities below by writing the number of the scripture verse beside the word. More than one verse may apply.
For example, Trustworthy-verse 11, 12

1. **Trustworthy**
2. **Reverent**
3. **Wise**
4. **Industrious**
5. **Benevolent**
6. **Accomplished**
7. **Rare**
8. **Confident**
9. **Resourceful**
10. **Valued**
11. **Commended**

1. Can you think of any additional words to describe a person of virtue? Write them beside the verse in the lesson.

2. This woman knew how to "handle her business." What do you and this woman of virtue have in common? Which of these qualities applies to you? List them and write one or more sentences describing how. Example: Benevolent- volunteering at a homeless shelter etc.

3. Which traits are challenging?

4. Review verses 28-31. What are the benefits of being a person of virtue?

5. Think about developing into a virtuous individual like the one we have studied. Is this a realistic goal for you? Please be specific in your answer.

6. How will you begin to incorporate more of these virtuous qualities into your own life?

Walk It Out

~ Reflect on your relationship with the Lord. Commit to honor Him more.

~Allow today to be the beginning for developing **your** potential. Use *Philippians 4:13* to pray and believe God to work virtue in you.

Declare this: I have the strength to face all conditions by the power that Christ gives me.

LESSON 2

AUTHENTIC

Genuine; true; in opposition to that which is false, fictitious, or counterfeit

Growing up, whenever my mom prepared spaghetti and meatballs, it came out of a can. I loved it because it was all I had experienced at that time. When I grew up and actually had fresh pasta, sauce and homemade meatballs, there was no going back to the canned product.

However, the availability of imitation food products, costume jewelry, and name brand knock off clothing make it tempting to settle. Those things may look good and taste okay until there is an opportunity to experience the real thing.

Though you may or may not have a preference when it comes to food, jewelry or clothing, relationships are a different story. I don't know of any person desiring fake relationships, yet, so often people wear facades pretending to be something they are not. In the words of music legends Nick Ashford and Valerie Simpson, "Give me something real."

Perhaps people are reluctant to show or share their true selves due to a fear of rejection, criticism or judgment. No matter the reason for falsehood, Jesus nonetheless advocated being genuine by walking in truth. In John 14:6, Jesus said He was the truth. Truth denotes honesty, sincerity and uprightness.

As Jesus was loving, compassionate and kind, He was also forthright and unpretentious. Jesus was secure in His identity and sure of the assignment He received from God the Father. Therefore, as Jesus was in the earth, we are to be also because God created us to be like Himself from the beginning.

Genesis 1:26-27 (CEV)
26. *God said, "Now we will make humans, and they will be like us. We will let them rule the fish, the birds, and all other living creatures."*
27. *So God created humans to be like himself; he made men and women.*

Psalms 8:5 (CEV) *You made us a little lower than you yourself, and you have crowned us with glory and honor.*

The sin of disobedience caused a rift between God and humans. (Read **Genesis 2:15-3:23**)
The man and woman were no longer carefree. They could not stay in the beautiful garden nor enjoy the intimacy of God's presence any more.
They died to the life of God that day.
Genesis 3:23 GNB *So the LORD God sent them out of the Garden of Eden and made them cultivate the soil from which they had been formed.*

Due to God's unconditional love, He made a way for our reconnection, reconciling us to Himself.
1 John 4:10 GW *This is love: not that we have loved God, but that he loved us and sent his Son to be the payment for our sins.*
Romans 6:23 GW *The payment for sin is death, but the gift that God freely gives is everlasting life found in Christ Jesus our Lord.*

Scripture reveals to us that all who believe in and receive the Lord Jesus become God's offspring.

John 1:12-13 ESV
12 *But to all who did receive him, who believed in his name, he gave the right to become children of God,*
13 *who were born, not of blood nor of the will of the flesh nor of the will of man, but of God.*

Therefore, we should operate in truth whether or not we feel it gives us an advantage or places us in an unfavorable light with people. Being our authentic selves pleases God, so it is worth the risk.

Psalms 51:6 GNB *Sincerity and truth are what you require; fill my mind with your wisdom.*

John 17:17 GW *"Use the truth to make them holy. Your words are truth.*

John 8:31–32 GNB
31 *So Jesus said to those who believed in him, "If you obey my teaching, you are really my disciples;*
32 *you will know the truth, and the truth will set you free."*

God is the author of truth.

Psalms 119:160 (CEV) *All you say can be trusted; your teachings are true and will last forever.*

Conversely, lies and deceit originate with Satan (better known as the devil). The moment we choose to lie, manipulate, or speak insincerely, we move over into Satan's realm of darkness.

John 8:44 GW *You come from your father, the devil, and you desire to do what your father wants you to do. The devil was a murderer from the beginning. He has never been truthful. He doesn't know what the truth is. Whenever he tells a lie, he's doing what comes naturally to him. He's a liar and the father of lies.*

Choose to be authentic in all of your relationships and in business dealings. Speak the truth in love wherever you go.

Work It Out

~ Using the information from lesson 2, please complete the following sentences.

1. _____ is another word for authentic.

2. God created _____ to be like Himself

3. The sin of _____ caused a rift between God and man.

4. God's love for us gave _____ as
_____ for our sins.

5. According to *Psalms 51:6* God requires _____
and _____.

~Answer the questions below.

1. Who is the author of truth?

2. Who is the father of lies?

3. Where do we find truth?

4. From **John 8:32**, what happens when we know and
embrace the truth?

5. Why do you think it is important to be authentic?

Walk It Out

~Reflect on what it means to be authentic.

~Are you satisfied with the level of authenticity in your relationships?
What areas need to be improved?

~Remember that truth is essential in maintaining a right relationship
with God and others.

I pray that you will become more authentic and unafraid to be true to who God has called to you be and to what He wants you to do.

Declare This: I am a child of God and will live a life of integrity and truth.

LESSON 3

LOVE

Show kindness to somebody; affectionate concern for the well-being of others

When you hear the word love, what are your first thoughts? Maybe the picture of a couple walking hand-in-hand comes to mind or perhaps your spouse, child or other family members do.

Classic songs like "All You Need is Love," "Love Makes the World Go Round," "What the World Needs Now is Love," and "Love is a Many Splendored Thing" among many others, express the prominence of love in our society.

Love is a little word with many definitions and **tremendous** significance! It is a word often misunderstood, misrepresented, and tossed about with reckless abandon. Yet, it is what we all need to experience and demonstrate to add meaning to our lives.

There are three different types of love. There is **Eros,** a Greek noun that refers to desire and sexual attraction. It is where the word erotic comes from. Often referred to as love, this "feeling" or attraction can come and go depending on the circumstances.

Phileo is also a Greek word used to describe a glow of the heart stemming from a response of a person to what he or she finds enjoyable or pleasurable. For example, when I say, "I love butter pecan ice cream or romantic comedies," mean I enjoy them a great deal. Another use of the same word depicts warm, friendly love and brotherly kindness, attachment and affection. It is the basis or root for the word philanthropy.

The last type **Agapan,** a Greek verb, is really the meat of our study

Linda S. Norwood

on love. It refers to deliberate choice. In the Bible, it is a relationship of self-giving.

This kind of love does not rely on the emotions. God demonstrated this to us through Jesus' sacrificial death on the cross to cancel our sin debt, and it is what He continues to show us day by day. God's love is steadfast and faithful.

As Christians, we are not only encouraged but are required to demonstrate this love. It is our greatest commandment.

Matthew 22:37-40 GNB
(37) Jesus answered, "Love the Lord your God with all your heart, with all your soul, and with all your mind.'
(38) This is the greatest and the most important commandment.
(39) The second most important commandment is like it: 'Love your neighbor as you love yourself.'
(40) The whole Law of Moses and the teachings of the prophets depend on these two commandments."

Observations

Verse 37-38
-Loving God with everything in us is our first priority

Verse 39
-Loving ourselves is next in importance, and then love others

Verse 40
-Obedience to the love command fulfills the law

Let's Chat

There is no question that we are to love God and put Him first in all things. What I found interesting was the link between loving ourselves with others.

62

The assumption is that everyone loves himself or herself but the truth is, not everyone does. The person that cannot seem to get along with anyone probably has an issue with his own self-perception.
When we do not love ourselves, it is very difficult to love others.
Loving yourself is not being self-centered; it is recognizing that you, though human, are a way God has chosen to express Himself in the earth, and therefore are valuable. Scripture tells us that if we do not love others, we do not really love God.
Love when demonstrated, fulfills the law (Ten Commandments) because it is so powerful and complete.

Understanding that love is paramount is great, but what does a lifestyle of love really look like and how are we to demonstrate love to others?
Given the previous definitions, sometimes it is easier to grasp what the God kind of love is by first knowing what it is not.

I Corinthians 13:1-8a AMP

¹IF I [can] speak in the tongues of men and [even] of angels, but have not love (that reasoning, intentional, spiritual devotion such as is inspired by God's love for and in us), I am only a noisy gong or a clanging cymbal.

²And if I have prophetic powers (the gift of interpreting the divine will and purpose), and understand all the secret truths and mysteries and possess all knowledge, and if I have [sufficient] faith so that I can remove mountains, but have not love (God's love in me) I am nothing (a useless nobody).

³Even if I dole out all that I have [to the poor in providing] food, and if I surrender my body to be burned or in order that I may glory, but have not love (God's love in me), I gain nothing.

⁴Love endures long and is patient and kind; love never is envious nor boils over with jealousy, is not boastful or vainglorious, does not display itself haughtily.

⁵It is not conceited (arrogant and inflated with pride); it is not rude (unmannerly) and does not act unbecomingly. Love (God's love in us) does not insist on its own rights or its own way, for it is not self-seeking; it is not touchy or fretful or resentful; it takes no account of the evil done to it [it pays no attention to a suffered wrong].

⁶It does not rejoice at injustice and unrighteousness, but rejoices when right and truth prevail.

⁷Love bears up under anything and everything that comes, is ever ready to believe the best of every person, its hopes are fadeless under all circumstances, and it endures everything [without weakening].

⁸Love never fails

Observations

Verse 1-3
- Language; knowledge/insight; miracle working faith; sacrificial giving to help others, mean nothing unless motivated by love

Verse 4a Love:
- waits with a good attitude

Verse 4b Love does not:
- give up but stays put
- want what someone else has
- consider self better than others

Verse 5 Love is not:
- stuck-up
- selfish
- thin skinned
- keeping score of hurts

Verse 6a Love does not:
- find pleasure in the unjust treatment of others

Verse 6b Love is:
- happy with the truth
- happy when the right thing is done

Verse 7a Love is:
- steadfast and unwavering in every situation

Verse 7b Love:
-   chooses to see the good in others
-   expects good things
-   persists in spite of difficulties

Verse 8a Love:
-   wins every time

Let's Chat

These particular scriptures are essential for me because with the stuff of life, it is too easy to deplete my love reserve. Therefore, I must continually refuel by reading and meditating on these verses.

I am a work in progress with a desire for a perfect heart toward God who has loved me through many struggles and issues. One major problem was with keeping my thoughts and attitude in check. There were times that the least little thing said to me by a particular person rubbed me the wrong way, and I made sure to let the person know it. Yet, I loved God or at least thought I did.
However, this is what **1 John 4:8 -12 (CEV)** says.
God is love, and anyone who doesn't love others has never known him.
The Lord gently showed me that if I truly loved Him I had to love others, which included a right heart attitude toward that person. The scriptures on love were very eye opening and convicting because they revealed the resentment I allowed to build up in my heart. I had to deal with it by acknowledging it was sin and dishonored God. Next, it was important to ask for and receive His forgiveness. (I John 1:9) Then repentance was necessary, meaning I had to change the way I thought about it.
Operating in the God kind of love is pure, being opposite of our "natural" instincts. Natural instinct says, "They hurt me, so I will get back at them!" Love says, "Although they hurt me, I choose to forgive them."

Yes, the love God requires us to display is a matter of choosing to forgive, help someone or show kindness because God has demonstrated this to us. It is not easy, but we have help from His Holy Spirit!

Realizing I did not have to feel "warm fuzzies" to walk in love set me free. I began to trust the Holy Spirit to help me do what was right by faith, not by feelings. The more I allow God to change me, the easier it becomes to love from a pure heart. I can love on purpose.

So where are you in this process?

Work It Out

~**Review I Corinthians 13:1-3. In your own words write out what the verses mean.**

~**Read the following scenario. Write out whether it reflects love or natural instinct and why below.**

"I have to be out for a while," Myra called out to her husband Milton as she was leaving.
"Okay, bring me back a sub sandwich," he responded.
Myra snapped," Why should I? You didn't bring back the milkshake I asked for last Tuesday."

How can Milton and Myra avoid a potential argument? Identify and write the scripture verse that will help.

~Read the sentences below. Place a *Y* beside the ones that demonstrate love and write an *N* beside the ones that do not. Think about why they do or do not demonstrate the biblical definition of love.

___ I will give some clothes to Goodwill because I really need a tax break.

___ My car is a luxurious red Lexus. What kind of car do you drive?

___Let me help you put up the groceries.

_____ As it began to rain, Charles ran to share his umbrella with Sandra.

__ "You are so stupid!" Candace thought to herself, looking in the mirror.

Walk It Out

~Read these additional scriptures on love.

Mark 12:33 (CEV) It is also true that we must love God with all our heart, mind, and strength, and that we must love others as much as we love ourselves. These commandments are more important than all the sacrifices and offerings that we could possibly make."

1 John 3:23 (CEV) God wants us to have faith in his Son Jesus Christ and to love each other. This is also what Jesus taught us to do.

1 John 4:8 –12 (CEV) God is love, and anyone who doesn't love others has never known him. 9) God showed his love for us when he sent his only Son into the world to give us life. 10) Real love isn't our love for God, but his love for us. God sent his Son to be the sacrifice by which our sins are forgiven.
11Dear friends, since God loved us this much, we must love each other.
12 No one has ever seen God. But if we love each other, God lives in us, and his love is truly in our hearts.

~Why do you suppose there is great emphasis on love throughout scripture?

~What area(s) challenge you most: loving God, people or yourself?

~Write about it and ask the Lord for the grace to express love His way.
I pray that you will love God, yourself, and others more.

Declare This: Because I embrace God's love for me, I am able to love myself and freely extend His love to others.

LESSON 4

> ## UNIQUE
>
> *Existing as the only one;*
> *having no like or equal;*
> *distinctively characteristic*

In **Genesis 1:26**, we learned that God made humans in His image. One outstanding characteristic of God is His uniqueness. There is no comparing Him to another. He, Jehovah, is the only true living God.

Isaiah 46:9 GW *Remember the first events, because I am God, and there is no other. I am God, and there's no one like me.*

In the same way, God uniquely created us to be unique. Each human being is distinctively different amid commonality. For example, each person's fingerprint including those of identical twins is unique to them.

Like fingerprints, no one else is like you. You have a particular way of doing things. Your personality is distinct as is the way you think and process information.

Every person is born uniquely designed by God for a specific purpose. For that reason, there is no need to become envious or jealous of another's ability or resources. God has gifted each person with what he or she can handle, including trials.

I Corinthians 15:10a (CEV) But God was kind! He made me what I am and his wonderful kindness wasn't wasted.

Ephesians 2:10 GNB God has made us what we are, and in our union with Christ Jesus he has created us for a life of good deeds, which he has already prepared for us to do.

Observations

I Corinthians 15:10a
- God's kindness has made us what we are

Ephesians 2:10
- God specifically created us to accomplish good things in this life through Christ Jesus

Let's Chat

The preceding scriptures reinforce this truth: not only did God create us, but He also created all that we are and will become. All of the skill we gain; things of high quality we achieve in this life, are through our union with Christ Jesus because of His marvelous plan for us.

All of the credit for the good things we do goes to God because of His Holy Spirit working within us.

Philippians 2:13 ESV for it is God who works in you, both to will and to work for his good pleasure.

God prepared for every contingency.
Peek a little more into God's purpose for His unique creations.

1 Peter 2:9 KJV *But ye are a chosen generation, a royal priesthood, an holy nation, a peculiar people; that ye should shew forth the praises of him who hath called you out of darkness into his marvellous light:*

I Peter 2:9 GW *However, you are chosen people, a royal priesthood, a holy nation, people who belong to God. You were chosen to tell about the excellent qualities of God, who called you out of darkness into his marvelous light.*

Romans 12:2 GNB *Do not conform yourselves to the standards of this world, but let God transform you inwardly by a complete change of your mind.*

Then you will be able to know the will of God---what is good and is pleasing to him and is perfect.

Romans 12:2 GW *Don't become like the people of this world. Instead, change the way you think. Then you will always be able to determine what God really wants-what is good, pleasing, and perfect.*

Romans 12:2 MSG *Don't become so well-adjusted to your culture that you fit into it without even thinking. Instead, fix your attention on God. You'll be changed from the inside out. Readily recognize what he wants from you, and quickly respond to it. Unlike the culture around you, always dragging you down to its level of immaturity, God brings the best out of you, develops well-formed maturity in you.*

Observations

I Peter 2:9
- God has chosen and set us apart for Himself
- He brought us out of darkness into His amazing realm of light
- our words of praise and actions are to rehearse and reflect God's excellent qualities

Romans 12:2
- we are not to blend in with the world but stand out
- dramatic change occurs from the inside out as our thoughts line up with God's Word
- we are able to recognize God's perfect will

Let's Chat

In reality, few people are comfortable with standing apart from the crowd. Many make a point to blend in and "go with the flow." How many brilliant ideas and creativity will go unrecognized because of the fear of sounding foolish or appearing strange?

I believe it is important to create an environment where people can embrace their own uniqueness along with the uniqueness of others as God intended. Each person is an individual; yet, our distinctions combined make a beautiful masterpiece and testify to the greatness of God. Therefore, as God's peculiar or unique people, we are to display righteousness, joy and peace. He has called followers of Christ out of the mundane spiritual darkness of this world's system, into His radiance or as scripture calls it, His marvelous light.

The Encarta's chief definition of light is God being a source of spiritual illumination and strength. Other definitions include energy producing brightness; to make it possible or easier to understand something; to reveal something.

Renowned physicists Albert Einstein and Max Planck studied light and developed theories pertaining to what it is and how it travels, etc. The study of light continues today, expanding previous theories. However, all theories verify that without light, nothing would exist.

1 John 1:5 GW *This is the message we heard from Christ and are reporting to you: God is light, and there isn't any darkness in him.*

Science confirms the truth of God's word pointing man back to His Creator, because God is the author of all that holds universe in place.

Psalms 19:1b GW ...The heavens declare the glory of God, and the sky displays what his hands have made.
Without God, nothing would exist!

The definition of darkness, on the other hand, includes absence of light; miserable (characterized by unhappiness, misfortune, or pessimism); nasty (evil or wicked; closed; uninformed).

Satan uses tactics to keep people in the dark about the consequences of sin. A lifestyle of sin separates us from God. Notice the very definitions of darkness characterize life apart from God.

I remember how miserable and unsatisfied I was before surrendering every aspect of my life to the Lord. Total surrender allows us to experience a deeper love relationship with Him. As I spend time getting to know the Lord, He helps me understand myself more, appreciating who He created me to be.

My desire is that you, too, will come to know yourself in Christ learning to embrace and appreciate your uniqueness.

Work It Out

~Read and answer the questions below.

1. Are you a people pleaser? If so, tell why and how.

2. On a scale of 1 to 5, how comfortable are you with yourself?

3. Has someone ever said that you were different? If so, what was the occasion? How did it make you feel?

4. Do you view being unique as positive or negative? Please explain your answer.

5. Think of three or more ways your uniqueness can be an asset in your sphere of influence.

Walk It Out

~Reflect on being unique.

~Remember God created you uniquely to fulfill His plan and purpose. Do not allow the enemy or others pressure you into trying to live someone else's life. God knows who you are and where you are.

Embracing your uniqueness and that of others starts with developing a relationship with Jesus through the study of His Word. Take the time to discover and explore the gifts and abilities God has placed in you. Ask the Holy Spirit to help you use them for the welfare of others and God's glory.

I pray you will recognize and embrace the worth and value of your own uniqueness.

Declare This: I am learning to enjoy who God uniquely created me to be!

LESSON 5

> ## ABIDE
>
> *To dwell, rest, continue, stand firm, or be stationary for anytime indefinitely.*

Abide is an old English word with different meanings used in early translations of Hebrew and Greek text, in what we know today as the Old and New Testament. Although the use of the word may be infrequent, its meaning remains very pertinent to our lives on many levels. In this lesson on abiding, we will study passages of scripture, which are the hallmark of the Christian life. We will learn in whom to abide along with how to abide as we delve into the Word.

The King James Version of the Bible, one of the earliest translations published in 1769, is still widely read today. This is how **John 15:4 KJV** reads.

*Abide in me, and I in you. As the branch cannot bear fruit of itself, except it **abide in** the vine; no more can ye, except ye **abide in** me.*
A more current reference or use of the word abide is to live in or stay united to.

Other translations using contemporary speech have been made available that are more reader friendly and easier to understand without compromising the integrity of the Holy Scriptures.
Look at these different translations of John 15, verse 4.
The words in bold print replace abide.

*GW **Live in** me, and I will **live in** you. A branch cannot produce any fruit by itself. It has to stay attached to the vine. In the same way, you cannot produce fruit unless you **live in** me.*

*GNB **Remain united to** me, and I will **remain united to** you. A branch* *cannot bear fruit by itself; it can do so only if it **remains in** the vine. In the same way you cannot bear fruit unless you **remain in** me.*

*(CEV) **Stay joined to** me, and I will **stay joined to** you. Just as a branch cannot produce fruit unless it **stays joined to** the vine, you cannot produce fruit unless you **stay joined to** me.*

The vine Jesus refers to in **John 15** is a grape vine. When researching grapevines, I saw pictures of branches growing out from a thick vine, which looked like a small tree trunk, strong and sturdy. Branches attached or connected to the vine produced lush clusters of grapes. Jesus used this vivid depiction to express the significance of abiding in Him for productivity in life.

Jesus' teaching reveals the way to lasting fulfillment and true success. These truths are what many people without a real relationship with Jesus are investing much of their time, energy and resources to find out through self-help books and "success" gurus.
Can people really find the way to lasting fulfillment and true success without Him? Review the text for the answer.
John 15:4 GW *Live in me, and I will live in you. **A branch cannot produce any fruit by itself.** It has to stay attached to the vine. In the same way, **you cannot produce fruit unless you live in me.***
John 15:5 GW *"I am the vine. You are the branches. Those who live in me while I live in them will produce a lot of fruit. **But you can't produce anything without me.***
According to these verses, fruitfulness/true success will not occur apart from Jesus.

The first three words in **John 15:4** contain a directive "Live in me," then the assurance, "and I will live in you". The remainder of the verse gives the reason for the directive. I love the fact that all of God's commands/directives regardless of how they appear are always for our good. God is not a megalomaniac taking delight in holding His power over our heads. He knows all things desiring what is best for us.

Jesus abides in the person who abides in Him, which causes fruit production. Bearing fruit corresponds with making progress, getting results or becoming successful while staying connected to Him.

On the other hand, goals and dreams we aspire to achieve in our own strength apart from the Lord, often fall short and are unrealized. They wither and die as a branch disconnected from the vine, its source of nourishment and life.

John 15:6 GNB *Those who do not remain in me are thrown out like a branch and dry up; such branches are gathered up and thrown into the fire, where they are burned.*

I remember the pear trees my dad planted in our yard. Not once did I observe pears growing on branches that had fallen to the ground separated from the tree. The branches, for whatever reason dropped off becoming dry and brittle. In turn, the rotting fruit dropped off because the branches, apart from the tree could not retain the life that once flowed through them. Branches that have no life, have no purpose so they dry up.

Jesus (the true vine) is the source for lasting fulfillment and success. Remaining in Him means staying in close fellowship with Him, allowing His Zoe to operate within us, which brings about positive results. Zoe is a Greek word used in the New Testament to specify the Devine eternal life of God.

However, living apart from Him eventually triggers dissatisfaction and despondency, which left unchecked, limit a person's effectiveness in his or her environment.

John 15:7 GNB *If you remain in me and my words remain in you, <u>then you will ask for anything you wish, and you shall have it.</u>*

Jesus' bold promise of receiving whatever we ask for is with the condition of staying united to Him allowing His Words to become apart of us. Although a directive, we have to exercise our will to abide during the most difficult circumstances. When we are disappointed and want to quit, Jesus reminds us that reward awaits the person who will stick with Him.

However, God is not a genie, Santa Claus or errand boy. He is sovereign over the entire universe, being supreme in power and dominion, not ruled by anyone or anything apart from Himself. He does what He knows is best in the way that is best; so, while those who abide in Jesus can ask with the assurance of receiving their request, I have learned that the timing of the answer and the method of answering is entirely God's choice.

John 15:8 GNB *My Father's glory is shown by your bearing much fruit; and in this way you become my disciples.*
Jesus explains that the productivity and success of God's people display the glory of God the Father because He receives honor and great praise. When we do things to advance the kingdom of God, we are following Jesus' example. Jesus Himself said in **John 14:12a GNB** *I am telling you the truth: those who believe in me will do what I do- --yes, they will do even greater things....* WOW! That is hard to imagine but is true because Jesus said it. Jesus' three-year earthly ministry, though short, was highly effective. He accomplished all that the Father assigned to Him because:

1) He knew His purpose- **Luke 4:18 GNB** *"The Spirit of the Lord is upon me, because he has chosen me to bring good news to the poor. He has sent me to proclaim liberty to the captives and recovery of sight to the blind, to set free the oppressed...,* **John 10:10 GNB** *The thief comes only in order to steal, kill, and destroy. I have come in order that you might have life--life in all its fullness.*

2) The Holy Spirit empowered Him - **Luke 4:18a GNB** *"The Spirit of the Lord is upon me...;* **John 1:32 (CEV)** *I was there and saw the Spirit come down on him like a dove from heaven. And the Spirit stayed on him.*

3) He stayed in communion with God the Father- **Luke 5:16 (CEV)** *But Jesus would often go to some place where he could be alone and pray.*
Likewise, people of God accomplish much through abiding in His Son, Jesus. Through Him, we discover our purpose, are empowered by the Holy Spirit and have ongoing communion with God as we abide. Whatever the assignment or challenge, we can accomplish it because we can do all things through Christ, who strengthens us. (**Philippians 4:13)** The word Christ translated from the Hebrew word *Mashiah* or *Messiah* into Greek is the New Testament designation for Jesus. Christ means anointed of God, chosen and set apart for His specific plan and purpose. It is where the word Christian derives.

John 15:9 GNB *I love you just as the Father loves me; remain in my love.*
Jesus is in whom His followers are to abide, and love is the way to
abide. Love is what sets those who follow Jesus apart from the world.
*(John 13:35 GNB) If you have love for one another, then everyone will
know that you are my disciples."* The love Jesus talks about here is
unconditional, not based on emotions.
Love's demonstration is through acts of kindness and compassion,
more concerned with the welfare of others.

John 15:10 GNB *If you obey my commands, you will remain in my love,
just as I have obeyed my Father's commands and remain in his love.*
How can we abide by remaining in Jesus' love? Simply obey what
He says. Study the Word and expect the Holy Spirit to help you do
it! Since Jesus obeyed the Father God's commands, our obedience
is necessary if we are to do what Jesus did. Therefore, abiding is the
lifestyle of a true follower of Jesus.

Work It Out

~ **Answer the questions below.**

1. 1. According to John 15:4, what is required to have a
   fruitful life?

2. Who is the true vine?

3. How can a person stay connected to Jesus?

4. What does being fruitful mean to you?

~Read the sentences below. Place a *T* beside true statements and an F beside false statements.

____Fruit continues to grow on branches detached from trees.

____Jesus is the true vine.

____God wants us to bear little fruit.

____ The key to abiding in Jesus' love is through obedience to His Word.

____Answered prayer is a result of staying united to Jesus.

____Emotions are an accurate demonstration of **real** love.

Walk It Out

~Reflect on what it means to abide in Jesus as the true vine.

~Are you satisfied with your fruit?

~Meditate on John 15:7-10.

I pray that you will purpose to cultivate a lifestyle of abiding in Jesus today.

Declare this: I will accomplish great things, as I stay united to Jesus!

LESSON 6

> ### BALANCE
>
> *A state of equilibrium; mental steadiness or emotional stability*

Every so often, I use a large ball to test my balance while exercising. To stay balanced requires concentration and continual adjustment to my placement on the ball. Depending on my balance that day, I may have to steady myself often by quickly planting both feet on the floor to avoid falling.

The strategy to achieving balance whether in exercise or managing situations in life is not placing too much weight in one area. When weight is not <u>equally distributed</u>, it becomes difficult to find stability. Without stability, whatever you are trying to balance will topple.

Living a balanced life, though challenging, is definitely worth the effort. Some principal factors to consider while on the quest for balance are prioritizing/placement and moderation/quantity.

Moderation refers to using sound judgment to avoid excess. You have heard the saying, "all work and no play makes Jack a dull boy. The truth is that **all** work and **no** play will make Jack an unhealthy boy.

Too much of anything, even something good (like work), has the potential of becoming a detriment. If you have a family, investing the majority of your time at work on a regular basis is not wise.

Finding balance is to know when enough is enough.

Balancing activities that involve work, home, church, and so on, are essential to function daily in a healthy way. How well we achieve and maintain balance determines the quality and can affect the quantity of our lives in a real way. Still, each person will actualize balance differently as each person is unique.

God knew that we needed balance and established the principle for it. According to **Ecclesiastes 3:1-8,** there is a time for all things. However, we need the wisdom of God to know what activities to get involved in, and the degree of involvement we should have in them. Because of God's goodness, we do not have to fear entrusting every aspect of our lives to Him. It is His desire for us to live well and to take pleasure in living.

1 Timothy 6:17b GW *.... Instead, they should place their confidence in God who richly provides us with everything to enjoy.*

Psalms 84:11 GNB *The LORD is our protector and glorious king, blessing us with kindness and honor. He does not refuse any good thing to those who do what is right.*

In "*VALUABLE Part I, Discovering Your Value,*" we learned that we are spirit we have a soul and live in a body. Since God created us in this triune fashion, He has provided His Word to make us aware and help us understand how to take care of each area. Therefore, we must know the Word in order to utilize it to achieve balance in our spirit, soul, and body, thus promoting wholeness.

Body
With our *body*, we make contact with and interact in the world by the use of five physical senses of taste, touch, smell, vision, and hearing. It is what we need to operate effectively in the earth.
Yet, the body in its current state will not live forever being composed from dust (**Gen. 2:7**). It will eventually die and return to the dust.

Read these scriptures regarding the body.

1 Corinthians 6:19 (CEV)
You surely know that your body is a temple where the Holy Spirit lives. The Spirit is in you and is a gift from God. You are no longer your own.

1 Corinthians 6:20 GW
You were bought for a price. So bring glory to God in the way you use your body.

1 Corinthians 9:27a ESV
But I discipline my body and keep it under control....

Romans 6:12-13 GW

12 Therefore, never let sin rule your physical body so that you obey its desires.

13 Never offer any part of your body to sin's power. No part of your body should ever be used to do any ungodly thing. Instead, offer yourselves to God as people who have come back from death and are now alive. Offer all the parts of your body to God. Use them to do everything that God approves of.

Proverbs 3:7-8 MSG

7 Don't assume that you know it all. Run to GOD! Run from evil!
8 Your body will glow with health, your very bones will vibrate with life!

Psalms 127:2 MSG

It's useless to rise early and go to bed late, and work your worried fingers to the bone. Don't you know he enjoys giving rest to those he loves?

Psalms 127:2 GNB *It is useless to work so hard for a living, getting up early and going to bed late. For the LORD provides for those he loves, while they are asleep.*

Observations

---

1 Corinthians 6:19-20
- our body is a temple where the Holy Spirit lives
- the Holy Spirit is a gift from God
- we no longer belong just to ourselves
- it cost God to purchase us
- the use of our bodies should bring God glory

1 Corinthians 9:27a
- our bodies need discipline

Romans 6:12-13
- don't allow sin's influence to dictate behavior
- give every part of the body to God exclusively for righteous purposes, never for ungodliness

Proverbs 3: 7-8
- relying on God's wisdom and turning away from evil Leads to life and a strong healthy body

Psalms 127:2
- working feverishly day and night is counter-productive
- God provides for those He loves as they rest

Let's Chat

The body of a person, who believes in the Lord Jesus and accepts Him as their Savior, is a temple of the Holy Spirit.

Because a temple is a holy dwelling, there is great significance in referring to our bodies as temples. God did not design our body to abuse drugs, alcohol, overeat nor live immorally. When we acknowledge the need for God's wisdom and choose to resist evil tendencies, our bodies respond in healthy ways.

According to the Word, I was purchased for God by the blood of Jesus, brought back from spiritual death to life, and I am no longer my own. I now realize that God is responsible for me. Psalm 127 confirms that I no longer have to try to figure things out on my own, or wear myself out trying to make something happen. I have a companion named Holy Spirit who is with me all the time, but is not intrusive. Since He lives in me, I depend on Him to help me take care of my physical body. I am encouraged to eat healthy, drink water, exercise and get the amount of sleep and rest that is right for me.

Soul
The soul, while sometimes interchanged with the spirit or heart, is distinct. It is where the activities of the **mind or intellect** (ability to think and reason), the **will** (exercising choice/making decisions), and **emotions** (what and how we feel) are governed. The soul is immortal.

The following scriptures address the soul.

Proverbs 17:22 GW *A joyful heart is good medicine, but depression drains one's strength.*

Matthew 6:31(CEV) <u>*Don't worry*</u> *and ask yourselves, "Will we have anything to eat? Will we have anything to drink? Will we have any clothes to wear?"*

Matthew 6:32 (CEV) *Only people who don't know God are always worrying about such things. Your Father in heaven knows that you need all of these.*

Matthew 6:33 (CEV) *But more than anything else, put God's work first and do what he wants. Then the other things will be yours as well.*

Philippians 4:6-8 (CEV)
6 <u>*Don't worry*</u> *about anything, but pray about everything. With thankful hearts offer up your prayers and requests to God.*
7 Then, because you belong to Christ Jesus, God will bless you with peace that no one can completely understand. And this peace will control the way you think and feel.
8 Finally, my friends, keep your minds on whatever is true, pure, right, holy, friendly, and proper. Don't ever stop thinking about what is truly worthwhile and worthy of praise.

Observations

Proverbs 17:22
- a positive attitude promotes health
- being negative depletes your energy/strength

Matthew 6:31-32
- Don't worry about your basic needs
- God is aware of everything concerning you

Verse 33
- When you put God first, you will have everything you need

Philippians 4:6-7
- do not allow anything to bother you or get on your nerves
- with thankful expectation, tell God everything you need and want
- remaining in Christ Jesus allows the peace of God to govern and stabilize your thoughts and emotions

Verse 8
- stay in control of your thought life; think on things worthwhile and true
- remember good things

Let's Chat

According to the American Psychological Association (APA), a survey released in January 2011, makes known deepening concerns about the connection between chronic disease and stress.
Chronic stress can affect both our physical and psychological well-being by causing a variety of problems, including: anxiety, insomnia, muscle pain, high blood pressure and a weakened immune system. Research shows that stress can contribute to the development of major illnesses, such as heart disease, depression and obesity. The consequences of chronic stress are serious.

While psychologists and others have been making this correlation over the years, God has always known it. (**3 John 1:2**)
It is for this reason He tells us repeatedly in His Word not to worry or become anxious/stressful, because what goes on in the mind greatly affects the body.

Proverbs 17:22 lays out what kind of attitude promotes good health and poor health. **Philippians 4:8** is specific in the types of thoughts that foster peace and wellbeing.
It is up to us to choose people, activities, and thoughts that are uplifting and purposeful. Continual worry and stress lead to depression.
Instead of holding things (problems) in, find a safe place to release

them. From experience, I know that God is the safest place there is. We can go to Him with any and everything. **1 Peter 5:7 (CEV)** *God cares for you, so turn all your worries over to him.*

God is concerned about the things that concern us and is big enough to handle all of our stuff! Having one or two trustworthy friends is also a blessing, when we need to vent and receive godly counsel.

I know depression can be quite debilitating depending on its type and severity, with different manifestations at various times. It may be thought that Christians walking with God should never become depressed, thereby causing feelings of guilt and shame when they are. If told, "walk by faith and receive your healing" some may be reluctant to seek treatment medical or otherwise. That type of thinking can put a person in bondage, which in turn prevents him from opening up to acknowledge that there is a problem, let alone seek help. While living by faith is paramount to the Christian, having faith in God for healing does not exclude doctors.

Learn to achieve balance by finding healthy ways to eliminate or manage stressful conditions instead of ignoring them.

Consequently, if you recognize as you engage in this study, that depression or other mental health concerns are an ongoing issue in your life, continue to trust God. Also do not be afraid to seek professional help from a physician, counselor, or receive psychiatric treatment.

God has many resources to help those in need. He provides according to each person's unique makeup, so again, keep your focus on the Lord and trust Him through the process of balance in your soul.

Spirit

Last, but most definitely not least, in our quest for balance is a look at a few scriptures relevant to our spirit.

The *spirit,* is very real, yet invisible, intangible and immortal. It is through our spirit that we connect with God.

Proverbs 20:27 ESV *The spirit of man is the lamp of the LORD, searching all his innermost parts.*

1 Corinthians 2:11 GNB *It is only our own spirit within us that knows all about us; in the same way, only God's Spirit knows all about God.*

1 Corinthians 6:17 GNB *But he who joins himself to the Lord becomes spiritually one with him.*

1 Corinthians 6:17 (CEV) *But anyone who is joined to the Lord is one in spirit with him.*

1 Thessalonians 5:23 (CEV) *I pray that God, who gives peace, will make you completely holy. And may your spirit, soul, and body be kept healthy and faultless until our Lord Jesus Christ returns.*

John 4:24 GNB *God is Spirit, and only by the power of his Spirit can people worship him as he really is."*

John 4:24 GW *God is a spirit. Those who worship him must worship in spirit and truth."*

Deuteronomy 6:5 GNB *Love the LORD your God with all your heart, with all your soul, and with all your strength.*

Observations

Proverbs 20:27
- God reveals things to us through our spirit

1 Corinthians 2:11
- Our spirit understands everything about us
- The Holy Spirit understands everything about God

1 Corinthians 6:17
- The person joined to the Lord is united Spirit to spirit

1 Thessalonians 5:23
- God wants us healthy in our spirit, soul and body

John 4:24
- God is spirit

- True worship takes place through our spirit by the Holy Spirit

Deuteronomy 6:5
- we are to love God with our entire being

Let's Chat

God communicates with us and reveals truths to our spirit by His Holy Spirit. I believe at times information conveyed to our soul (mind) results in our "a-ha" moments of inspiration. There are times when you know things that you really cannot explain. You just know that you know. Although developing a relationship with God is not a mental exercise, the will is engaged to choose to love and live for Him, knowing by faith we are one in spirit with Him.

The importance of taking care of the body and soul (physical and emotional well-being) is more apparent with the problem of stress and obesity escalating. Nonetheless, it is vital that the spirit is well nourished and healthy also.
To cultivate spiritual balance and health, first recognize that your spirit is the real you. Your body is your earth suit. I say your spirit is the real you because God is spirit (**John 4:24**) and He created you in His image and likeness. (**Genesis1:26**)

Staying in union with God through a lifestyle of worship includes fellowship by having conversations with Him, spending time in His Word, and enjoying times of praise to appreciate Him. Additionally, fellowship with others (particularly followers of Jesus Christ), engaging in fun wholesome activities that promote godly character (whether sports, movies/TV, reading and other positive things), is also incorporated into a lifestyle that honors God.

To complete our lesson on balance, I thought it would be interesting to get a medical doctor's perspective on living a balanced life, so

Dr. W. Whittaker from Atlanta, Georgia, was gracious enough to provide her feedback. This is what she shared.

The Lord is as concerned about our physical welfare as He is our spiritual welfare. The Bible says in 1Corinthians 3:16 that our bodies are the temple of the Holy Spirit. In 1Corinthians 6: 19-20, we are admonished to honor God with our bodies.

In everything, there should be balance. We cannot habitually eat junk foods and expect to be free from health problems.

Balance in life means:

Starting each day spending time with God
Eating the right foods
Exercising regularly
Forgiving so you can heal
Rewarding yourself for a job well done
Taking moments to smell the roses –"me time"
Living in the here and now
Getting regular health checks
Choosing to do manual labor or take a walk instead of smoking a
    cigarette when stressed
Doing random acts of kindness
Taking regular inventory of your life to see if you are walking in
    your destiny
Using every disappointment or failure as a stepping stone
Being TRUE to yourself
Maintaining an attitude of gratitude
Ending each day with reflection

Work It Out

~Review the lesson on Balance and answer the following questions~

1. What did the lesson reveal to you?

2. Three areas comprise our make-up as human beings. List
    them below.

    _____ , _____ , _____ .

3. Why should we take care of our bodies?

4. From Proverbs 17:22, what does a positive attitude provide?

5. God reveals things to our _____ .

~ **God created us spirit, soul and body. Reread Dr. Whittaker's
comments. Beside the activity, write the part spirit, soul, or
body that you feel is involved. One or more words may apply
to an activity.**

Walk It Out

~ **Reflect on and implement some changes that will promote
balance in your life~**

~Remember that we are spirit, soul and body **[1 Thessalonians
5:23]**. Each part is distinct, but whatever happens in one area affects
the other areas. Maintaining health and balance in each area will
determine the quality of life you will have and enjoy.
I pray that you will commit to loving the Lord with your entire being
and trust Him to help you develop a balanced lifestyle.

Psalms 84:12 GNB *LORD Almighty, how happy are those who trust
in you!*

Declare This: I will trust in the wisdom of God to help me live a
balanced life!

LESSON 7

Have you given thought to what you want to pass on to the next generation?

Maybe you think only the wealthy or affluent will have something to leave behind. I believe from the least to the greatest, whether intentional or not, we will leave something behind.

Will it be faith or fear, good character or an attitude of entitlement? Perhaps a gift of money will be left behind or possibly debt.

Will it even matter that you lived here on earth?

These are sobering questions requiring some thought.

Unfortunately, many people allow complacency to settle in merely existing from day to day not realizing they do have something worth passing on to the next generation.

On the other hand, if not careful, those of us endeavoring to live the abundant life Jesus came to give fall into the self-centeredness trap where the priority is "my ministry" and "my vision". The purpose of abundance is to have more than enough to help and inspire those we presently come in contact with, in addition to leaving something to help and inspire the ones coming after us.

Avoiding self-centeredness is necessary because leaving a legacy requires thinking beyond oneself.

Read what Proverbs has to say.

Proverbs 13:22 GW *Good people leave an inheritance to their grandchildren…*

According to scripture, one of the qualities of a good person is they leave a legacy or inheritance for their grandchildren, as well as their own children. I believe it is important that we purposefully live a life of quality that extends beyond us.

My grandparents, Joshua and Amy Dennis worked hard to raise four daughters and two sons in the early 1900s.
I remember my mother sharing that it was very important to Grand Dad that his girls were educated and in a position for self-sufficiency, married or not. As a result, all of the girls went to college and had careers in the field of education. My mother also developed a love for the Word of God and music as she and Grandma Amy spent time reading the Bible and singing together. My mother, in turn, sang to me when I was a child and prayed with me at bedtime. I have had a love for music ever since, and I have shared that love as well as my faith with my children. While my Grandparents were able to leave some land acreage for each child, they also left strength of character and other values worth much more.

How do you determine what the legacy to your children and grandchildren will be?
Here is a suggestion.

Deuteronomy 11:18–22 GW
18. Take these words of mine to heart and keep them in mind. Write them down, tie them around your wrist, and wear them as headbands as a reminder.
19. Teach them to your children, and talk about them when you're at home or away, when you lie down or get up.

20. Write them on the doorframes of your houses and on your gates.

21. Then you and your children will live for a long time in this land that the LORD swore to give to your ancestors-as long as there's a sky above the earth.

22. Faithfully obey all these commands I'm giving you. Love the LORD your God, follow all his directions, and be loyal to him.

2 Timothy 1:5 GW *I'm reminded of how sincere your faith is. That faith first lived in your grandmother Lois and your mother Eunice. I'm convinced that it also lives in you.*

Observations

In **Deuteronomy 11: 18-22,** God, through Moses, gives instructions to the Hebrew people after coming out of bondage to Egypt.

Verse 18
- take God's Word seriously
- do whatever is necessary to remember it

Verse 19
- use every opportunity to teach God's Word to your children

Verse 20
- keep God's Word visible at all times

Verse 21
- you and your children will enjoy longevity in the place God has promised

Verse 22
- love God and stick with Him
- follow all of His directions

2Timothy
Verse 5
- faith is transferrable generation to generation

Let's Chat

Although the commands outlined in **Deuteronomy 11:18-22** were directed to the Hebrew people, they are relevant to our lives today. **2 Timothy** reminds us of how expansive God's Word really is.

2 Timothy 3:16-17 (CEV) *Everything in the Scriptures is God's Word. All of it is useful for teaching and helping people and for correcting them and showing them how to live. 17) The Scriptures train God's servants to do all kinds of good deeds.*

So, all of God's Word is beneficial. It establishes us in truth, shows us what is good, and prepares us to practice doing what is right.

It also provides us with the guidance needed to live and enjoy a good quality of life. However, it is wise to treat God's Word as a vital necessity, then purpose to do what it says, being particularly mindful of our character. Character is extremely significant in as much as children watch and learn more from the way parents/guardians live rather than from what they say.

Teaching the Word of God to our children, allowing them to see our love and faith is truly a legacy worth more than all worldly wealth. Through His Word, we make wise investments into their future. Accordingly, it is up to parents/guardians to find creative ways to keep God's Word in the forefront at home demonstrating its continued relevance in daily life.

Work It Out

~ Read and answer the questions below.

1. How prepared are you to leave a legacy?

2. What do you feel was passed down to you?

3. If you could only leave one thing for the next generation, what would it be?

~Read the statements below. Write a T beside the True statements and an F beside the False. Write a sentence under each false statement that reflects the truth.

___ Only the rich and famous can leave an inheritance for their children.

___

___ A legacy is something passed along from past generations.

___

___ Good people leave an inheritance for their grandchildren.

___

___ Foolish people focus solely on the present.

___

___ God's Word is antiquated irrelevant.

___

___ Money is the most important thing to leave behind.

___

Walk It Out

~ **Reflect on what it means to leave a legacy.**

~Determine to be intentional as you live and interact with others each day. Believe you can make a difference in your environment.

~Use **Proverbs 13:22** to pray and trust God to develop His goodness in you.

I pray that your legacy will bless generations to come.

Make this declaration: As my life reflects God's goodness, I will leave an unforgettable legacy.

LESSON 8

> ## ENDURANCE
>
> *The ability or strength to continue or last, esp. despite fatigue, stress, or other adverse conditions; perseverance*

Additional words for endurance include staying power, patience, stamina, and determination. These words convey the attitude necessary to keep moving forward because the challenges experienced in life can be overwhelming and even debilitating. Yet according to scripture, we can be encouraged. Let's find out why.

In **John 16:33 GNB,** Jesus speaks this to His followers.
" *I have told you this so that you will have peace by being united to me. The world will make you suffer. But be brave! I have defeated the world!*"
Now read The Message translation.
John 16:33 MSG) *I've told you all this so that trusting me, you will be unshakable and assured, deeply at peace. In this godless world you will continue to experience difficulties. But take heart! I've conquered the world.*"

Observations

- trusting Jesus produces stability and peace
- all that live in the world will encounter trouble
- believers can have confidence because Jesus has conquered the world

---

Let's Chat

I would love to tell you that when you accept Jesus as your personal Savior, study His Word and are obedient to what He says, your life becomes trouble-free. However, I cannot do that, because it would not be the truth according to what Jesus revealed here in the gospel of John.

One of the many things I love about Jesus is His candidness. Though gentle, He never sugarcoated anything.

He revealed that there would be suffering and hard times while living in the world, but He also provided hope and encouragement.

What is the world? The world Jesus referred to in this scripture, is from the Greek word "cosmos," meaning "world-system."

Satan has a heavy influence upon the "world system," which is demonstrated by the wickedness seen and encountered on a daily basis. He is called the god of this world as found in **2 Corinthians 4:4 (CEV)**.

The god who rules this world has blinded the minds of unbelievers. They cannot see the light, which is the good news about our glorious Christ, who shows what God is like.

Other scriptures that refer to Satan are the following:

John 12:31 GNB *Now is the time for this world to be judged; now the <u>ruler</u> of this world will be overthrown.*

John 14:30 (CEV) *I cannot speak with you much longer, because the <u>ruler</u> of this world is coming. But he has no power over me.*

Ephesians 2:2 GW *You followed the ways of this present world and its <u>spiritual ruler</u>. This <u>ruler</u> continues to work in people who refuse to obey God.*

1 John 5:19 GW *We know that we are from God, and that the whole world is under the control of <u>the evil one</u>.*

It may be unpopular, but it is clear from the previous verses that Satan is real and is the temporary ruler of this world's system. People who refuse to receive the good news concerning the deity of Jesus, His death, burial and resurrection, have their minds blinded by him. It is also clear that Satan works in all who fail to obey God. However, Jesus thoroughly conquered Satan and his demonic world-system at Calvary.

1 John 4:4 (CEV) *Children, you belong to God, and you have defeated these enemies. God's Spirit is in you and is more powerful than the one that is in the world.*

Those who accept Jesus as Savior and Lord are able to overcome every obstacle, problem, or challenge thrown at them in the world. Still, remember the key to living in victory hinges on staying united to Jesus, relying on the Holy Spirit who lives within us.

One way to view successful Christian living is as a long distance race (marathon) and not a sprint. Marathons require endurance and if we desire to experience the victory Jesus has provided, we must be prepared to hang in there for the long haul, believing in His ability to sustain us.

1 John 5:4 (CEV) *Every child of God can defeat the world, and our faith is what gives us this victory.*

2 Corinthians 2:14 ESV *But thanks be to God, who in Christ always leads us in triumphal procession, and through us spreads the fragrance of the knowledge of him everywhere.*

Faith is an essential component of endurance. We have assurance of overcoming the trials and tribulations of this world because of the Spirit of God living in us.
We have to believe what God says through His Word and maintain a positive attitude.

Another reason to be encouraged in spite of trials is that **they have purpose.**
Romans 5:3b-4 GW
…We know that suffering creates endurance, endurance creates character, and character creates confidence.

Romans 15:4 GW *Everything written long ago was written to teach us* so that we would have confidence through the endurance and encouragement which the Scriptures give us.

James 1:2 (CEV) *My friends, be glad, even if you have a lot of trouble.*

James 1:3 (CEV) *You know that you learn to endure by having your faith tested.*

James 1:4 (CEV) *But you must learn to endure everything, so that you will be completely mature and not lacking in anything.*

James 1:12 (CEV) *God will bless you, if you don't give up when your faith is being tested. He will reward you with a glorious life, just as he rewards everyone who loves him.*

James 1:12 GNT *Happy are those who remain faithful under trials, because when they succeed in passing such a test, they will receive as their reward the life which God has promised to those who love him.*

Hebrews 10:35 GW *So don't lose your confidence. It will bring you a great reward.*

Hebrews 10:36 GW *You need endurance so that after you have done what God wants you to do, you can receive what he has promised.*

2 Corinthians 4:17 GNB *And this small and temporary trouble we suffer will bring us a tremendous and eternal glory, much greater than the trouble.*

Observations

Romans 5:3b–4
Suffering builds:
- endurance
- character
- confidence

Romans 15:4
Scripture provides:
- confidence through endurance
- encouragement

James 1:2
- endurance fosters maturity
- staying confident is a choice
- being confident brings reward

James 1:3
- endurance increases through the testing of faith

Hebrews 10:35-36
- endurance and confidence make God's promises reality

2 Corinthians 4:17
- God's glory is eternal and greater than the temporary issues we face

---

Let's Chat

According to scripture, the problems, suffering and or trials we encounter have purpose. Paul goes as far as to say that we should be happy when we have trouble, counting it all joy. Honestly, in my most spiritual of moments, I have not clapped my hands with glee and shouted, "Yea trials!" Not many people are happy during their trials.

However, understanding the purpose of suffering has helped me to have a better attitude while going through.

While I do not like to suffer, admittedly much of my spiritual growth takes place as I endure various hardships. Just as the scripture says, trouble forces me to grow up in many ways.

Suffering and trials develop spiritual strength in a Christian's life, just as resistance training helps to develop ones strength physically. Resistance training is a bit uncomfortable but is a needful part of the process. Understanding that trials are a part of the process to grow and develop spiritually, aids in our preparation to endure.

Sometimes the person training will enlist the services of a personal trainer. The personal trainer shares their expertise, provides instruction, encouragement and support to the individual as they train to achieve their desired goals. As Christians, we also have a wonderful personal trainer in the person of the Holy Spirit. The great thing about Him is that He is with us all of the time because He resides in us. He never needs to take a break.

God's Word also provides the encouragement we need to assist us as we endure. In it, we find examples of great people who placed their trust in God, were confident in His faithfulness, persevered through trials and were victorious.

We, too, develop confidence in God as He sustains us in the middle of difficult circumstances. Still, we must choose to hold on to our confidence in Him, not becoming discouraged when situations take a **long** time to change.

Galatians 6:9 KJV *And let us not be weary in well doing: for in due season we shall reap, if we faint not.*

Our enemy Satan uses fatigue and discouragement, hoping we will give up and quit on God, life and ourselves. While Satan's intent is to frustrate and debilitate us with trouble, we can rest assured that God's purpose is to build us up so we can receive His great and precious promises.

Genesis 50:20a GW *Even though you planned evil against me, God planned good to come out of it.*

The more we trust Him through trials, the more He reveals His all-sufficiency, building our confidence in Him even more. As we endure and achieve victory, healthy self-confidence builds up within us. I feel good about myself when I refuse to quit and am able to see God work as only He can. How do you feel?

Romans 8:28 GNB *We know that in all things God works for good with those who love him, those whom he has called according to his purpose.*

I encourage you to trust in the wisdom of God at all times, including the extremely difficult seasons. Remain steadfastly confident in His good purpose as you learn to endure.

Work It Out

~Review the lesson on Endurance to answer the questions below~

1. Spiritual growth takes place through _____.

2. Why can Christians experience joy in trouble?

3. What do trials accomplish?

4. How can we remain confident during a trial?

Walk It Out

~Reflect on the benefits of endurance~

~Remember to thank the Lord for spiritual growth during times of adversity.

I pray that your confidence in the Lord remains intact through every trial and that you develop the strength to encourage others.

Declare This: My confidence in God brings great reward!

There are many uncertainties in this life.
God's love for you is not one of them.

You are VALUABLE!

Notes

Notes

CONCLUSION

God has a favorable view of you. Be empowered through His Word to live a victorious life of virtue knowing your worth. Speak words of life to others because God has accepted you to abide in Him. Maintain a positive self-perception by receiving God's unconditional love. In return, love Him, yourself and people unconditionally. Become secure in your identity because God understands the unique person that you are. The fearfully wonderfully way God made you is affirming, so do not be afraid of becoming authentic in every area of your life. When God placed inside us the things that make us tick, His intent was and is for us to experience blessing and balance in our spirit, soul and body. You can choose to enjoy the liberty Jesus provided, while leaving a legacy to encourage and benefit those coming after you. Finally, the fact that you are still alive is an expression of God's grace, kindness and mercy. Remain confident as you endure life's challenges. God will reward your trust in Him.

On A Personal Note: "VALUABLE" is a testament to the faithfulness of God. It is also a reflection of my personal journey in overcoming feelings of inadequacy, to become comfortable in my own skin. As I prayed and studied the Word, God provided comfort and courage, enabling me to believe in the reality of His unconditional love for me. The book **"VALUABLE"** began to unfold, resulting in an ability to love and believe in myself again with a clear call to comfort others, as I had been comforted. (**2 Corinthians 1:3-4**)

It has been a privilege to share God's love and His comfort.

You are **VALUABLE**

ABOUT THE AUTHOR

Linda S. Norwood is an anointed Bible teacher and praise and worship leader. Linda also serves in several ministerial capacities often as encourager and mentor to women.

Her years of experience in public education as a teacher and administrator, honed her ministry as a Bible teacher. Linda has taught Bible studies throughout the greater Atlanta metropolitan area, ministered the Word of God at various churches and conducted workshops in Georgia and South Carolina. She has also published numerous articles in her blog, **heavensdew.blogspot.com** to encourage the heart and refresh the soul.

In addition to new authorship, Linda is a singer and songwriter. In January of 2009, Linda released a debut CD titled "Eternal Praise". The inspirational project well received continues to bless many hearts. **Eternal Praise is available for purchase on iTunes or visit, www.cdbaby.com/LindaNorwood.**

Linda prays that through her inspirational writing, teaching and songs, people will be encouraged in the Lord Jesus and experience His unconditional love; learn to love Him through intimate fellowship; love themselves embracing their own uniqueness; and genuinely love others.

Linda currently lives in Georgia with her family.

VALUABLE Information
Linda S. Norwood

Her services include:
- VALUABLE Workshops
- Keynotes
- Praise and Worship Encounters

To leave a testimonial contact Linda at the following:
Email: lindasnorwood12@gmail.com
Phone: 678-744-6584

Follow Linda on Twitter:
@be_refreshed
Like her on Facebook/Valuable

Source Notes

Part I- Discovering Your Value

Preface
American Psychological Association, April 2010 study on self-esteem
http://www.apa.org

Chapter 1
Encarta Dictionary English (North America)
Online, "valuable" p. 3

Chapter 7
Encarta Dictionary: English (North America)
Online, "accept" p. 25

Webster's II New Riverside Dictionary, "salvation" p. 25

Part II- Insight and Reflections

Unless otherwise identified, all definitions in the acronym VALUABLE are from Merriam-Webster's Collegiate Dictionary (Eleventh Edition)

Webster's 1828 Dictionary, "Grace" p. 39

Part III- Learn and Grow
Unless otherwise identified, all definitions in the acronym VALUABLE are from the Encarta Dictionary: English (North America)
Online

Lesson 1
Webster's II New Riverside Dictionary, "Virtue" p. 44

Lesson 3
Wuest's Word Studies in the Greek New Testament, "Eros", "Phileo", "Agapan" p.55

Lesson 4
Dictionary.com Online, "Unique" p.63

Lesson 5
Webster's 1828 Dictionary, "Abide" p. 69

Lesson 8
Dictionary.com Online, "Endurance" p. 93